Fitness Training for Girls

A Teen Girl's Guide

to Resistance Training,

Cardiovascular Conditioning

and Nutrition

Katrina Gaede
Alan Lachica
Doug Werner

Illustrations by Cristina Martinez
Photography by Doug Werner

Tracks Publishing
San Diego, California

Fitness Training for Girls

*A Teen Girl's Guide to Resistance Training,
Cardiovascular Conditioning and Nutrition*

Katrina Gaede / Alan Lachica / Doug Werner

Tracks Publishing
140 Brightwood Avenue / Chula Vista, CA 91910
619-476-7125 / www.startupsports.com

Publisher's Cataloging in Publication

Gaede, Katrina.
    Fitness training for girls : a teen girl's guide to
    resistance training, cardiovascular conditioning and
    nutrition / Katrina Gaede, Alan Lachica, and Doug Werner. --
    1st ed.
       p. cm.
    Includes bibliographical references and index.
    LCCN: 2001093706
    ISBN: 1-884654-15-0

    1. Teenage girls--Health and hygiene. 2. Physical
fitness for women. I. Lachica, Alan. II. Werner,
Doug, 1950- III. Title.

RA777.25G34 2001   613'.04243
                      QBI01-201131

To
My Mother and Father
Dawn and Carl Gaede

Acknowledgements

Erin Morse

Phyllis Carter

Michelle Devilliers

Personalized Workout

Tammy Parsons

Ken Type

Pam Drucker

Janet Patry

Sue Hyde

Your very own personal trainer

 We wanted to produce a guide that would truly serve all girls. Our programs are based on athletic training programs and speak directly to teens interested in sports. But we want to make it clear that these workouts will also benefit those whose primary goal is to begin a life of higher fitness and stay there.

This is nothing new — the body is a temple for your mind and spirit. Develop and care for it and you will enrich everything else in your life. Learn that now when you are young. It is so much more difficult when you grow older. Just look around you!

Consider this book your very own personal trainer. That's what we had in mind when we began this project and sure enough, everything in these pages is repeated in our gym and our lives every day.

Believe in yourself and the power of physical fitness to lift your life. Here's to you!

Katrina
Alan
Doug

Contents

A life of fitness

Fitness training: for sport, for well-being, for life

A fitness guide just for teen girls

Teen girls interested in serious fitness training programs have little to choose from on the bookshelves.

> Gaining optimum physical well-being is no longer an exclusive athletic ideal. The benefits of fitness training can enhance the lives of all girls.

There are lots of books about self-esteem, pimples and boyfriends but few substantial workout guides. This book will tell you how to get athletically fit and firm — using the gym or making do at home — for sport and a sporting lifestyle.

Training for athletes and everyday girls, too!

Fitness Training for Girls sounds serious. It's that second word that does it. By definition training is the process or state of being formed by instruction, discipline and drill. Anything that involves all that must be pretty serious, indeed. So it makes sense that this is a book for athletes or aspiring athletes. Athletes train. That's what they do.

But *Fitness Training for Girls* is for all the other girls, too. Or at least the ones who wish to attain fitness that goes beyond dieting and exercising to lose weight. They may not have the talent or desire to be athletes,

but they want to achieve and maintain a life of fitness all the same. The processes for both athletic and non-athletic girls take earnest effort and the processes overlap — especially in the beginning. Fitness is not exclusive. It is achievable for every girl who wants it.

Muscles are OK
In 1972 the U.S. Congress enacted the Educational Amendment Act. Title IX of that Act requires that colleges and universities who want to keep government funding must provide students with equal opportunity in all areas of college life, including sports.

The need to field more women's athletic teams fueled the development of high-school and recreational sports for girls. Girls' high-school teams increased from 15,000 to 70,000 in the '80s and women's sports participation increased 700% overall.

Girls' athletic participation coincided with, and no doubt encouraged, our society's growing interest with fitness over the last two decades. As a result, the female body ideal that includes soft, full curves made room for a powerfully new and vibrant option — the athletically fit and muscularly toned body type. Once scorned for being unfeminine, athletic adolescent girls gained respect and admiration for their healthy bodies.

What's real: The myth of the perfect body
It should be enough to say that physical perfection is not an option — because it does not exist. Although we are seduced by a narrow standard of beauty through magazines, television and film, what we admire is the behind-the-scenes work of cosmetic professionals and digital touch-up. Trying to look like the girl in an ad is futile. More importantly, it's the wrong place to start your dream. You must begin with you.

Every girl has her own unique body. There are things you like, things you're OK with and things you dislike. The idea is to accept what you have, improve what can be improved and take pride in your very best efforts.

> ## Strength to succeed is in your head.

Comparing yourself to others or photos in magazines ignores who you are and what your needs are. Instead of envying pixels on the page or screen, look to your own improvements as you reach the goals that will take you to your dreams.

**You CAN! Eliminate quitter's mentality
— Gain mental toughness**
Building and maintaining fitness is a lifestyle. It's about making better choices regarding eating and exercise every day of your life. For a healthy, happy life. For a remarkable life.

Fitness training is not easy. Nothing worth doing or achieving ever is. But it is doable — even in the beginning. When the simplest exercise is so difficult — you can complete one more rep. Even when your desire for certain foods seems overwhelming — you can think it through and make a wiser choice. Strength to succeed is in your head. You can if you think you can. That's what we mean by mental toughness.

It's easy to find reasons to quit on yourself. Exercise can be hard and boring and sweaty — why punish yourself? Doing what you want when you want is more like it — why deny yourself? Giving up and giving in can seem appealing. So appealing that you may acquire "quitter's mentality" and never try. But without trying there can be no success at anything. Quitting is just, well, quitting.

The first step is the hardest
For those who have never tried, getting
past the comfort zone is the biggest
challenge of all. Each of us live
day in and day out in a
personalized bubble.
In the bubble we are
comfortable, when we make an
effort to break out of it, we are
not. Exercise includes a certain
amount of discomfort and difficulty and it is most acutely felt
in the very beginning. That's
when the desire to quit can
wash over you like a big wave.

**Triumphs will
see you through**
Mental toughness is about seeing
yourself through initial discomfort
and consequently overcoming the
desire to quit again and again and
again. It's about challenging yourself.
It's about proving something to yourself.
When hurdles are overcome, the triumphs of each
small victory build inside you and they leave a mark.

There comes a point when you will begin to seek challenge and relish the opportunity to overcome difficulties. You will discover that the triumph of reaching
each goal far outweighs any discomfort you endured to
get there.

Rewards: Big returns for big effort

It's important to know that fitness training grows on you. It always gets better and you will learn to enjoy it more and more. You are blessed with a forgiving body that will respond gloriously to serious sustained effort and care. In other words, there will be rewards for working out and eating right.

It is only natural that actions you repeat will become habits. One fine day you will realize that all those habits have built a new you. That's the way it works. It's that simple. All you have to do is try each day. And the harder you try, the greater the reward.

FTG 1

Fitness is key

Physical, emotional and mental well-being — the undeniable connection to fitness

I don't like what I see!

Is this a secret? Teen girls are self-critical. Physical changes within yourself and among friends naturally fosters an interest in what you may see in the mirror. Yet if you seriously compare yourself to models or celebrities in the magazines and movies (or anyone for the matter) that interest turns into an unhealthy concern. As a result you may, for example, seek to be ever thinner. Good eating habits go out the window and exercise is just a way to lose calories.

> All that stuff you have heard about eating right and exercising — how it's so good for you, how it makes you feel better, how it can improve so many things in your life now and in the future — it's true.

What's wrong with that picture?

Nobody's perfect

As mentioned earlier, the celebrity look is not real — it's the result of cosmetics, staging, lighting, even surgery. Photos and video are usually touched up. Perfection does not exist!

Making unhealthy choices
An obsession with thinness will induce you to make unhealthy choices. It is irrational to believe that success is largely determined by standards of weight, body shape and facial characteristics.

It's about you
It's important to understand at an early age that well-being is born and nourished from within. It begins by learning to accept who you are and by taking good care of yourself.

I'm a nobody!
Studies have shown that girls feel pretty good about themselves until they reach high school. Then doubt sets in as well as struggles with self-esteem. What causes the downshift?

Making comparisons
Girls become externally focused. They begin to wonder what others think of them, especially peers and, of course, boys.

You may ask yourself *Am I attractive to those around me? Do I rate with them?* Instead of *How do I feel inside? Am I feeling strong and vibrant?*

Expectations from above
About the time girls develop individuality, they still feel pressure to conform to behavioral standards set by parents, teachers and other adults. As a result they may feel torn, confused and anxious.

**Self-esteem is a
choice you can
make right now!**
Raising self-esteem can
begin by making healthy
choices — eating right
and exercising. A
healthy body paves
the way toward
forming a strong
self-image. Developing
and managing a fitness
program
for your-
self is an
excellent
way to learn
how to set
goals and reach
them. Feeling
better enables you
to grow comfortable
with yourself and the world around
you. It becomes easier to work and
play and relax. You'll smile and laugh
more!

Seven reasons to eat right and get fit
All that stuff you have heard about eating
right and exercising — how it's so good for you,
how it makes you feel better, how it can improve
so many things in your life now and in the future
— it's all true.

1. Enhance physical development

Eating right and exercising will strengthen your immune system — you'll get sick less. You'll build stronger bones and muscles and develop healthier heart and lungs.

2. Gain mental acuity

You'll experience better focus and memory.

3. Reduce stress

Exercise helps eliminate anxiety.

4. Build self-esteem and self-confidence

No doubt about it — exercise and a proper diet will make you feel good and look good!

5. Enjoy deeper sleep

Sleep will come easier after a day with exercise.

6. Live a longer and healthier life
Healthy habits you develop today will reduce the risk
of heart disease, obesity, high blood pressure, some
forms of cancer and other health problems.

7. Meet new and healthier friends
You'll find like-minded girls working out in the gym,
running the trails or playing between the white lines.

Being positive

Adolescence is often blue. Or it can seem that way. Discover that a healthy body feeds a vibrant spirit (and vise versa).

Staying positive and puberty, too

Of course it's hard to stay positive all the time!

Your body is developing on a fast track — hormones are flowing and emotions are intense. Add peer pressure, parental expectations, school and work and you have a mess of stress. Feeling confused, uncertain and inadequate at times is normal during the transition from girl to woman.

As a teen girl, you are in for your fair share of ups and downs. Working out and eating right will help immensely in the long and short term.

Puberty

A girl's first period often happens around age 12 or 13. But it's not uncommon for individuals to have it as early as 10 or much later in her teens.

Physical changes are radical but normal. They include growing taller, increased body fat, larger breasts and weight gain around the hips and stomach. A week before a period you may get premenstrual syndrome (PMS) and suffer irritability, fatigue, cramping and melancholy (the blues).

It can be a difficult time but it's important (and comforting) to remember that you are not alone and talking about it with friends and parents may help. All girls go through puberty. You are simply becoming a women.

Exercising and eating right really help!
Working out releases anxiety and actually produces a chemical that positively influences mood and energy. A healthy diet provides energy and helps level emotional ups and downs.

Positive thinking
There's a lot of peppy advice for those singing the blues these days and that's a good thing. Much of it revolves around the concept of enjoying the moment, which of course, is exactly what we should be able to do all the time!

The problem is taking it to heart when you feel down! So if you can't make yourself feel better by thinking positive (not a lot of people can) at least you can fake it until you make it. That is, just keep on keeping on ...

Accept that bad things happen and move on
Probably the most important part of a healthy attitude is how you react after a setback. The answer is simple, but the battle you wage within your mind and heart

It's important to know that you have the power to make things better.

after a disappointment may not be. Losing can get personal. It can make you feel like nothing. It can hurt.

The answer is to try again and keep at it despite the emotional pain. You must believe that things will improve — and you must always believe in yourself.

If you can dream it you can do it.

Believe in yourself, face your fears and never give up.

2
weights
stretch
3
bike
stretch
4
weights
run
5
9
weights
run
stretch
11
bike
weights
12
17
19
25
26

Goals

About making plans, setting a course for yourself and keeping track of your progress

Develop a plan

It helps enormously to have a master plan that encompasses your dreams with steps to make them come true. Give yourself plenty of time and break it down by month and week.

Make long-term goals and short-term goals. A plan should include a structure you believe in and can live with. Then it will imbed itself in your mind and become an important part of your life. Without a plan your workouts will become pointless and whimsical, like any other careless endeavor, and you will not stick with it.

> *Patience is important. Work toward your goal gradually — not too much too soon. Don't quit before you've had a chance to experience the reward of exercise.*

For example, a simple, yet effective master plan might include a promise to yourself to develop the 10 core body parts and muscles discussed in this book. For 6–8 weeks straight you will exercise each of those 10 muscles twice a week using the exercises shown. This is your long-term goal.

Keep a chart to document progress

Decide what exercises you want to do each day of the

week and write them down on a chart. Each day record how many reps and sets you completed and how much weight you were using. Keep the chart in a prominent place so you can't hide it from yourself.

The idea is to make the chart and daily exercise a dynamic part of your life — *something you just gotta do!* Completing the exercises you set for yourself each day and week are your short-term goals (and checking them off as you complete them is a sweet part of the day!)

Keep a journal
Writing daily about your new life of fitness forces you to take your efforts seriously and to think clearly about what you are doing. You simply cannot write about anything without really thinking about it first. Writing will crystallize your thoughts and help make vital what you are doing.

This is not just "Dear Diary" stuff. Keeping journals about important passages in one's life is a powerful and proven way to understand oneself better. Write about your fitness and progress, of course, but tackle all the outside stuff that affects you, too. Bad things are brought to light when you write about them and it can help a great deal to vent.

Visualize
Create and keep visual ideas of your successes in your mind. Start each exercise with thoughts of successful execution. And store visions for what you seek over the long term, too.

Visualization is the first step you take in any journey. Imagining yourself conquering goals — victorious and vibrant — feeds a winning and healthy attitude about what you are doing. It also blocks out distractions and everyday negativity coming from others or the dank crevices of your brain.

Your mind is more powerful than you probably know. Your success, your fitness, your well-being is between the ears. Once you truly know that and learn to train your thoughts — absolutely nothing will stop you.

Plan, guide and motivator

To the right is a **sample** workout chart for a week. It shows days for resistance training and cardiovascular conditioning with stretching before each session.

A chart like this (you will develop your very own) is a plan, a guide and a motivator — unless you hide it in the bottom of a drawer.

This is an example only! ⟶

Further explanation of the workouts in this chart will be presented in chapters 5, 6 and 7–7.3.

Monday	Stretching	Stretch body parts below and running muscles			
	Core Muscle Develop	Upper leg / step-up DB	2 sets	12 reps	5 lbs
		Thigh front / squat DB	2 sets	12 reps	10 lbs
		Thigh back / lunge DB	2 sets	12 reps	5 lbs
		Chest / chest press DB	2 sets	12 reps	10 lbs
		Upper back / pullover DB	2 sets	12 reps	15 lbs
	Cardio	Run 30 minutes	one sentence / one breath		
Tuesday	Stretching	Stretch body parts below			
	Core Muscle Develop	Low back / prone back raise	2 sets	12 reps	
		Abdominal / crunches	2 sets	12 reps	
		Shoulders / overhd press DB	2 sets	12 reps	5 lbs
		Up arm frnt / biceps curl DB	2 sets	12 reps	8 lbs
		Up arm bk /triceps kickbk DB	2 sets	12 reps	5 lbs
Wednesday	Stretching	Stretch running muscles			
	Cardio	Run 30 minutes	one sentence / one breath		
Thursday	Stretching	Stretch body parts below and running muscles			
	Core Muscle Develop	Upper leg / step-up DB	2 sets	12 reps	5 lbs
		Thigh front / squat DB	2 sets	12 reps	10 lbs
		Thigh back / lunge DB	2 sets	12 reps	5 lbs
		Chest / chest press DB	2 sets	12 reps	10 lbs
		Upper back / pullover DB	2 sets	12 reps	15 lbs
	Cardio	Run 30 minutes	one sentence / one breath		
Friday	Stretching	Stretch body parts below			
	Core Muscle Develop	Low back / prone back raise	2 sets	12 reps	
		Abdominal / crunches	2 sets	12 reps	
		Shoulders / overhd press DB	2 sets	12 reps	5 lbs
		Up arm frnt / biceps curl DB	2 sets	12 reps	8 lbs
		Up arm bk /triceps kickbk DB	2 sets	12 reps	5 lbs
Saturday	Stretching	Stretch running muscles			
	Cardio	Run 30 minutes			

And Sunday you rest — If you were to follow this program, in 6 days you would work each of the 10 core muscles twice. You would exercise 30 minutes within your target zone (using the one breath / one sentence method) 3 times. Note that stretching precedes each day's set of exercises.

Gym

Start looking for a gym by asking parents, a mentor or friends for suggestions of clubs in the area. Visit the facility and see if it meets your needs. Considerations include cost, equipment, classes, other friends that are members, atmosphere (is the place fun and vibrant?), service and attitude (are people smiling?).

In particular, look for a gym with upbeat, friendly, courteous, and informative employees who are willing to offer advice and help young people. Look for a variety of services for teens including group and personal instruction, and a wide array of classes to attend.

> *A good gym should provide proper gear and instruction. But it should also provide a stimulating atmosphere of purpose and camaraderie. The best gyms should motivate you!*

Usually clubs will offer a student discount, or you can be added to a family plan if parents are current members. Expect to pay from $12 to $50 per month with a possible enrollment fee. Most clubs will offer a special three-month summer plan. Personal trainers (other than this book) usually cost from $35 to $75 an hour.

Sign up at the front desk where you'll get instruction and information about the club, sign a contract and provide information as a new member.

What to wear

Wear gym attire that feels comfortable and that you can move around in easily. There is a wide range of fun, cute workout gear available. A good pair of tennis shoes is a must. They can be cross trainers or running shoes. Don't forget to keep long hair tied up and bring lots of deodorant! (Just kidding!)

Diving into the gym experience

A gym can be overwhelming and a bit intimidating at first — but everyone starts somewhere and you'll get into the mix soon enough. Working out with a partner or friend might be a good idea at first.

There will be people of all types and ages working out. Take classes right away to meet people and instructors and to get a feel for gym camaraderie. Use people around you to gather ideas about the gym experience.

In the gym you will develop a sense of awareness of your body physically, mentally and emotionally. It can be a great experience in an individual's life. So go for it, have fun, and remember you are doing it for yourself. And don't be afraid to make mistakes. The rewards are endless!

Finding a gym

Gyms should be easy to find. There are a number of family-oriented chain fitness centers to choose from, the YMCA and perhaps your high school.

Stretching

How to stretch your muscles before and after workouts and why you should

Stretching is an unsung cornerstone of fitness.

Although it doesn't have the appeal of other training programs, stretching reduces the chance of injury and helps keep joints and muscles flexible. When muscles are flexible you are able to reach, stretch and bend more easily.

Your flexibility is impacted by genetics, gender, age and level of physical activity. The more active you are, the more flexible you are likely to be. The good news is you can improve flexibility with regular training.

When to stretch

Serious flexibility training involves 30 minutes of stretching 3 times each week. If that's not feasible, it is important to stretch at least a few minutes before and after each workout (some is better than nothing).

Why stretch?
1. Improves range of movement
2. Improves posture
3. Reduces risk of injury
4. Relieves muscle tension and soreness
5. Provides physical and mental relaxation

Basic points of good stretching

1. The best time to stretch is when muscles are warmed up. Exercise large muscle groups to raise core temperature (body temperature) and get blood circulating. Warm up with a simple, low-intensity activity such as walking, light jogging, spinning or use of treadmill.

2. Stretch slowly.

3. Do not bounce.

4. Stretch the muscle to the point where you feel tension, not pain (stretching should not be painful!).

5. Breathe deeply throughout the stretch.

6. Hold for at least 10 seconds and then relax for 10 seconds. Repeat.

7. For maximum results stretch daily.

Stretching illustrated

Always stretch the muscle(s) you are going to work that day! Presented here are several stretches to get you going.

Lower back and hip stretch
Lie flat on back and flex one knee 90
degrees. With opposite hand pull
bent leg up and over other leg.
Opposite the pull, straighten
other arm and turn head.
Gently push knee to floor
to achieve stretch.
Repeat on other side.

Groin stretch
Sit erect on floor, flex
knees and place soles
of feet together.
Gently pull feet
toward you.

Groin and hip stretch
Sit with legs apart, arms extended and hands on floor. Slowly lean forward from hips to achieve stretch.

Hip stretch
Move one leg forward until knee is over ankle. Other knee rests on floor. Lower hip to achieve stretch. Switch leg postions and repeat.

Glute and hip stretch
Lie flat on back. Cross leg above knee at 90 degrees. Pull lower leg toward chest with hands clasped behind knee. Switch leg positions and repeat.

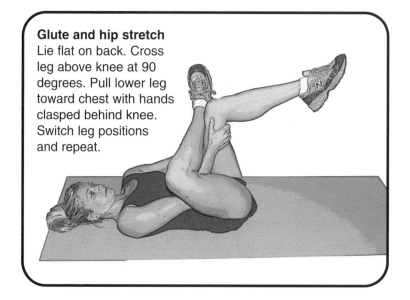

Lower back stretch
From a prone position push upper body from floor. Upper and lower legs in contact with floor throughout.

Calf stretch
Push against a wall with one leg extended behind. Extended foot is flat on floor. Repeat with other leg.

Achilles stretch
Follow instructions above for calf stretch and lift heel of extended foot. Repeat with other foot.

Hamstring stretch
Flex one leg and place hands
just above knee. Extend other
leg, resting weight on hands.
Keeping knee locked, push
down on heel of extended leg
to stretch calf and hamstrings.
Repeat with other leg.

Quadriceps stretch
Flex one leg at knee and
grasp foot with either
hand. Gently pull foot to
achieve stretch. You may
need to steady yourself by
leaning against a wall with
free hand. Repeat with
other leg.

Chest and shoulder stretch
Form a 90 degree angle at elbow joint with one arm. Place arm and hand flat against a perpendicular surface and push. Repeat with other arm.

Triceps stretch
Try to touch the small of your back with one hand. Gently pull the elbow with the other hand. Repeat with other arm.

Biceps stretch
Extend a straight arm and place hand flat against a perpendicular surface and push. Repeat with other arm.

FTG **6**

Cardio

About improving your
cardiovascular fitness
by exercising within
your target zone

> It's the time spent in your
> cardiovascular target zone that
> counts. Start out with 10–20 minute
> sessions 3–4 times a week and
> gradually increase the time (dura-
> tion) of each session.

**Cardiovascular
conditioning**
Your muscles need
oxygen to perform
properly after several

minutes of continuous exercise. Cardiovascular fitness,
or endurance, refers to how well your heart and lungs
pump oxygen-rich blood to your exercising muscles.

Cardiovascular activities are those that work the body's
largest muscle groups (larger muscles need larger
amounts of oxygen to perform) in continuous action. It
follows that regular cardiovascular exercise develops
endurance — specifically the capacity of your heart
and lungs to deliver oxygen to muscle tissue.

Cardiovascular activities (also known as aerobic activities — aerobic means "with oxygen") use leg and torso
muscle groups and include brisk walking, jogging,
swimming, cycling, rope jumping, rowing and certain
continuous action games like soccer.

Exercise within your target zone
The key to cardiovascular training is exercising within
your cardiovascular target zone. Each person has a cardiovascular target zone within which physical activity

must be maintained in order to build cardiovascular fitness. The target zone is measured by heart rate. Your target zone is 60-80% of your maximal heart rate.

Finding your zone
A simple way to determine your target zone is to subtract your age from 220 and multiply the difference by .60 and .80. The lower number gives you a target for an easy day. The higher number is your target for a hard training day.

For example, if you are 15 years old:

220 - 15 (years old) = 205
(205 is your maximal heart rate)

.60 x 205 = 123
(123 is the low end of your target zone)

.80 x 205 = 164
(164 is the high end of your target zone)

Wear a heart monitor
There is a very convenient way to check heart rate while exercising. You can purchase a wrist monitor (it looks like a wristwatch) and chest band that come as a set and wear them together during exercise. The set costs between $50 and $150. But if you find all this a bit technical try the ...

One breath, one sentence method
The simplest way to reach your target zone without formulas or gizmos is to exercise until you cannot speak a 10-12 word sentence without taking a breath.

For example, if you can recite the sentence *I'm reaching for my target zone and working hard to do it!* without huffing you are not there yet. If, however, you have to stop twice or more for air, you are beyond your target zone.

How long should I exercise?

In the beginning do no more than 20 minutes at a time. Take a conservative approach and train at a relatively low intensity — 50% to 70% maximum heart rate — for 10 to 20 minutes.

Your goal: We recommend you train at the high end of your target zone for at least 30 minutes 3-4 times a week.

Duration not intensity

A crucial component of cardio training is duration, which refers to the amount of time you spend exercising. Ideally, the session should vary from 20–60 minutes to gain cardio and fat burning benefits.

It's more effective to increase the duration rather than the intensity of your training. For example, if you are walking a treadmill, instead of increasing speed or making the incline steeper, go longer at the same pace to maximize the benefits of cardio exercise.

Cool down

Once you've completed your workout, spend about 5 minutes doing light stretches and taking deep breaths. Get out of your wet clothes and towel off.

NOT!

Resistance training

How to use your own body weight, free weights and machines to build and maintain muscles

Resistance training (a.k.a. strength or weight training)

As the name implies, in this type of training your muscles will be exercised against a resistance. Resistance in our programs will be provided by your own body weight, free weights (barbells and dumbbells), exercise machines and the

> **Relax! You will _not_ become a muscle-bound freak!** The idea that weight training will necessarily lead to an overly buffed, masculine physique is not true.

medicine ball. Stated simply, a muscle working at its maximum capacity will grow firmer and stronger as a result of increasing metabolic processes to handle the greater workload.

Why lift?

Strength training develops not only your muscles, but your bones, ligaments and tendons, too. Increased muscle mass makes you stronger, of course, but it also enables the body to burn more calories — even as you rest. Stronger bones, muscle and connective tissue decrease risk of injury and a toned musculature looks good on anybody. All this translates to greater overall well-being and self-respect.

Misconceptions:
Weight training and adolescent girls

Not so long ago weight training was not advised for young girls. It was thought there was significant risk of sustaining injuries to growth centers and musculo-skeletal systems. However, as stated previously, research over the last 20 years shows that weight training increases muscle strength and endurance, enhances the cardiovascular system and indirectly increases bone strength and self-esteem.

Relax! You will not become a muscle-bound freak!

The idea that weight training will necessarily lead to an overly buffed, masculine physique is not true. For the most part, weight training will not result in muscles that appear to be overproportioned.

How big your muscles become depends not only on the resistance program, but also on diet and especially on the amount of anabolic hormone (primarily testos-terone) in your system. Since females naturally have less testosterone than males, the muscle bulk girls develop, with properly applied resistance and good nutrition, will be considerably less.

When will you see a difference?

It's difficult to chart general fitness results. This is because of the many different body types and the way each individual body adapts to exercise. Girls' muscles react differently depending on a variety of factors including age, genetics, muscle fiber reaction and recruitment as well as the individual's previous sport and athletic involvement.

Having said that, if you have never trained seriously before you'll probably see rapid improvements in strength and muscle tone. Seeing definition for the first time is inspiring and you will need little else for encouragement. After a few weeks of working out, however, changes in strength and appearance will develop at a slower pace. You may want to seek motivation by joining a gym and working out with others.

Measuring progress
Your progress with free weights and machines is measured by the number of weight levels you advance. Advancing by 2 weight levels in each of the 10 core muscles is considered a significant gain.

Comparisons:
Training with your own body weight, free weights, and machines

Body weight training
This type of exercise involves using your body weight as resistance. Push-ups, pull-ups and sit-ups (crunches) are common body weight exercises. You can perform those and a number of other body weight exercises to  safely and effectively strengthen all the major muscle groups.

Keep in mind you must successfully execute an exercise in order to benefit. For example, if you cannot execute a proper push-up, do them on your knees until you have the strength to perform them on your toes.

Body weight training: positives
● Great for agility, coordination and muscle balance. A number of body parts get into the act. Muscles are not isolated. Surrounding muscles and connective tissues of the primary muscle(s) exercised are developed as well.

● Recruits and engages more muscle fiber per exercise than machines.

● Can be done anywhere, any time.

● Ideal conditioning for anyone.

Free weight lifting

Free weight training makes use of barbells and dumbbells. Barbell and dumbbells come in various shapes and sizes and may be adjustable (weight can be added or taken off) or fixed (weight is fixed to the bar).

Free weight training is more technical than other types of training. One must be sure exercises are performed correctly to maximize safety and results. Since movements are not fixed as on machines, you are more likely to perform the movement incorrectly. For some advanced free weight exercises, such as the squat, you need to develop abdominal and lower back strength before you add weight to the bar.

Free weight lifting: positives

● Effectively develops the helping or stabilizer muscles and connective tissue of the primary muscle(s) exercised. These are the muscles that stabilize one joint so a desired movement can be performed in another joint.

● Closely matches patterns associated with sport skills.

● Barbells and dumbbells are versatile, relatively inexpensive and take up little space.

● Effective in achieving overall strength.

● Develops important aspects of fitness such as size, flexibility, fat loss and muscle toning.

Free weight lifting: negatives
● Can be dangerous if you don't know lifting technique. Poor form can cause injury.

● If adjustable, weights must be carefully balanced and tightened.

● Does not achieve maximum isolation of muscle or muscle groups.

Weight machine exercising
Weight machines are easy to use because they provide a fixed movement pattern for each exercise and support for your body. Because some weight machines allow you to train specific muscle groups, you can also use them to isolate a muscle that may be weak or prone to injury.

Be careful when using machines because they are designed for adults. Improper positioning may result in your arm or leg slipping off the intended placement. Most machines will allow adjustment to insure proper fit. We believe that most types of machines can be safe for young people provided you follow appropriate guidelines (guidelines are usually posted on each machine).

Machine exercising: positives

● Effective in isolating a muscle or muscle group.

● Generally safer than free weights.

● Easier to use than free weights.

● Provides a faster workout.

● Generally better suited than free weights for an average fitness enthusiast.

Machine exercising: negatives

● Does not exercise stabilizing muscles (or stabilizers) necessary to develop proper muscle balance.

● Small girls may not fit some machines.

● Expensive to own.

How much weight should you lift?

Repetition range rule for free weights and machines

Take the time to discover your repetition range for each exercise. Say you want to perform 12-15 reps per set of each exercise. Make sure you can complete at least 12 reps in good form, but that 15 (or 14 or 13) complete reps is a struggle. If you can do more than 15 reps, increase the weight by a level. If you cannot do 12 reps, decrease the weight by a level.

Don't cheat! It's important to lift in good form without cheating (for example, swaying your back to perform a biceps curl) in order for training to be safe and effective!

About weight levels: A level is defined as the next closest measure of resistance for any given exercise. For example, a rack of dumbbells are often leveled (in pounds) 5, 8, 10, 12, 15, 20, 25, 30 and so on. Machines may have levels in increments of 10, 18 or 25 pounds each. It's a good idea to adjust your weights from one level to the next without skipping to best pinpoint your ideal weight for a given exercise.

How do I know if I'm getting stronger?
As stated previously, progress is measured by the number of weight levels you advance.

Doing it
About technique, reps, sets, frequency, rest and variety

Warm up and stretch before training

Exercise large muscle groups to raise core temperature (body temperature) and get blood circulating. Again, examples of good warm-up exercises include walking, easy jogging, spinning or use of a treadmill.

Lifting technique for free weights and machines

Exhale when you lift, push or pull resistance; inhale when you lower or release it. Lower or release the resistance with a slow, controlled motion. Lifting the weight to a count of 1-2 and lowering it to a count of 1-2-3-4 is works well.

Reps and sets

If you are beginning, we suggest no more than 2 sets of 12-15 reps per exercise at a very manageable weight (if using free weights or machines).

Terms defined

Repetition or rep:
A single exercise movement. Reps are usually done in multiples called sets.

Sets:
A group of repetitions done consecutively, without rest until a given number, or momentary exhaustion is reached.

Intensity:
Rate of performing work (a function of energy output per unit of time). Refers to the difficulty of a workout.

Frequency:
How often a person repeats a complete exercise session. Our programs suggest 2–3 times a week.

Duration:
The time spent in a single exercise session.

Sequence:
The order of muscle groups exercised in a workout routine.

As you progress, you will add weight, adjust the number of reps and increase the number of sets and sessions per week.

Rule of thumb (for free weights and machines): Fewer reps with more weight are performed to increase strength and muscle. More reps with less weight are performed to tone muscles or maintain what you already have.

Rest periods between sets

For endurance rest 30 seconds or less between sets. For strength rest 1-2 minutes between sets.

How often (frequency)

If you are just starting, you may want to perform only 1 session a week. Eventually, you will need to exercise each muscle group 2-3 times a week to yield results. Rest at least 1 day between workouts. Training more frequently or adding more sets may lead to slightly greater gains, but the small added benefit may not be worth the time, effort and risk of injury.

Importance of rest between sessions

It's just as important to rest as it is to work! Your muscles actually repair and build in the days after a workout. Exercise a particular muscle or muscle group no more than 3 times each week.

Some muscles need to be flexed first!

Make sure your workout program includes exercises that strengthen the trunk of your body — your abdominal and lower back. These muscles work as a unit to stabilize the trunk and keep it fixed during leg and arm movements. A poorly developed trunk provides little support for hard-working limbs.

Variety

Illustrated in this book are several ways to exercise the same muscles and muscle groups. It's important to mix up the exercises in order to combat boredom as well as the body's natural inclination to groove itself to a repeated task. Work your muscles different ways in order to keep workouts fresh and effective.

Cautionary notes

● Remember to work all the major muscle groups. Neglecting certain groups can lead to strength imbalances and difficulties with posture.

● Approach free weight lifting with caution. Make sure adjustable weights are tightened. Step up in weight level incrementally and carefully — especially with technically difficult exercises such as squats, step-ups and lunges. Use proper lifting technique.

● Drink plenty of water before, during and after working out.

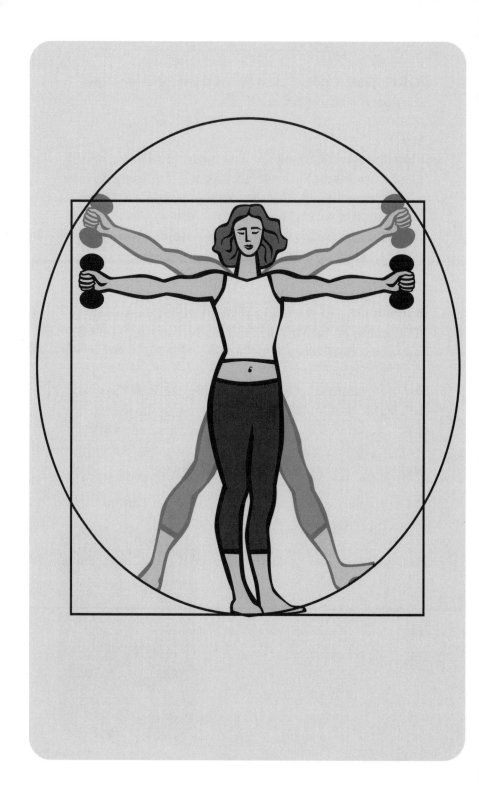

Core muscle strength training

Balance and strength

A well designed strength training program emphasizes balanced development of the major muscle groups. As stated in the last chapter, neglecting basic muscles can lead to strength imbalances and postural difficulties.

> *Core muscles include the major muscles of your trunk, shoulders, arms and legs. Exercise each of the ten core muscles 2–3 times a week to develop overall strength and symmetry.*

Our core muscle development program will build a broad base of muscle strength that should serve most of the athletic and personal goals of all girls. Furthermore, it is most important that you develop core muscles before initiating strength training for a particular sport or athletic event.

Core muscle development: 6–8 weeks

We suggest you perform an exercise that works each of the 10 major body parts and the corresponding muscles at least twice each week (some beginners may need to begin with only 1 session each week). Remember that each muscle or muscle group requires at least a day of rest between workouts.

The following several pages will show how to exercise each of the 10 core muscles using each of the 3 types of resistance: body weight, free weight and machine. Remember the workouts shown in this section are just a few examples of what you can do. There's a host of other exercises to try, and many are listed here and illustrated in this book later.

How long does it take?
In 6-8 weeks you should see significant development. The goal is to advance 2 weight levels with each of the 10 core muscles. At that time you may choose a sport-specific program or continue with general conditioning.

Core muscles to develop
Here are 10 major body parts and the corresponding muscles groups to be exercised for a general workout.

Body part	Muscle name proper / common
Upper Body, trunk 1. Chest 2. Upper back 3. Lower back 4. Abdomen	Pectoralis major (Pectorals/pecs) Latissimus dorsi (Lats) Erector spinae Rectus abdominus (Abs)
Shoulders and arms 5. Shoulders 6. Upper arm, front 7. Upper arm, back	Deltoids (Delts) Biceps (Bi's) Triceps (Tri's)
Lower body 8. Upper leg, back 9. Thigh, front 10. Thigh, back	Gluteus medius/maximus (Glutes) Quadriceps (Quads) Hamstrings (Hams/hammies)

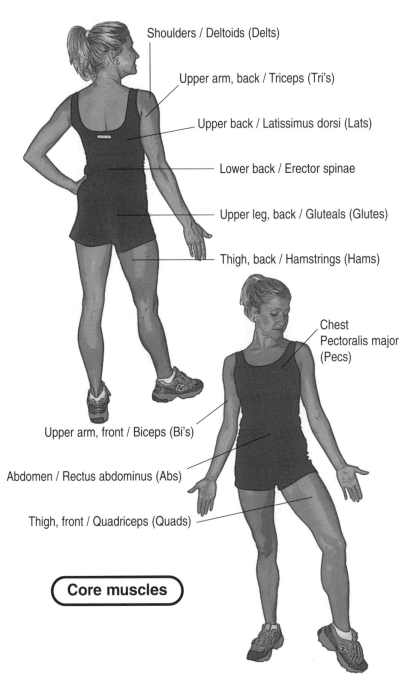

Shoulders / Deltoids (Delts)

Upper arm, back / Triceps (Tri's)

Upper back / Latissimus dorsi (Lats)

Lower back / Erector spinae

Upper leg, back / Gluteals (Glutes)

Thigh, back / Hamstrings (Hams)

Chest
Pectoralis major
(Pecs)

Upper arm, front / Biceps (Bi's)

Abdomen / Rectus abdominus (Abs)

Thigh, front / Quadriceps (Quads)

Core muscles

1. Chest: Pectoralis major (Pecs)

Body weight exercise: **Prone push-ups.** See also incline and decline push-ups and bar dips.

Free weight exercise: **Chest press** with dumbbells. See also chest press with barbell, incline chest press, chest fly and incline chest fly.

Machine exercise: **Chest press.** See also chest fly.

Prone push-ups

Lie on floor face down and position hands on floor in line with chest. With legs straight and toes on floor, push body up* with arms extended and body straight. Lower body back to floor without touching. Exhale as you push up and inhale as you come down.

1

2

*Push up from knees if you are not successful pushing up from toes.

Chest press with dumbbells

Lie on bench with knees up, feet flat and arms and weights extended straight up. Slowly bend elbows and lower weights to outside of chest. Press up until arms are fully extended. Head, shoulders and buttocks in contact with bench at all times. Hands positioned over elbows at all times. Exhale up, inhale

Chest press with machine

Back, butt and thighs fit snugly to seat. Feet are flat on platform. Knees flexed 90 degrees. Grasp bar and push slowly until arms are extended. Return. Inhale on return, exhale as you push out.

2. Upper back: Latissimus dorsi (Lats)

Body weight exercise: **Chin-ups**

Free weight exercise: **Pullovers** with dumbbell. See also pullovers with barbell and bent-over one-arm rows.

Machine exercise: **Front lat pulldowns.** See also seated rows and seated pullovers.

Chin-ups

With palms out, grasp bar and let body hang straight. Toes do not touch floor. Slowly pull up* until chin reaches bar. Return. Exhale up, inhale down.

*If you cannot execute on your own, have someone stand beneath you and provide push or use a chair or bench. Give yourself just enough help to complete reps you desire.

Pullovers with dumbbell

Lie on bench with knees up and feet flat. Hold one dumbbell with both hands and extend arms straight up. Slowly lower dumbbell overhead with arms straight until arms are parallel to ground. Return. Exhale up, inhale down.

1

2

Front lat pulldowns

Grasp bar with a wide overhand grip and sit with thighs under supports. Pull cable bar down under chin to upper chest until shoulder blades are squeezed together. Return until arms are extended. Exhale as arms come down and inhale as arms go up.

3. Lower back: Erector spinae

Body weight exercise: **Prone back raise.** See also
                        pelvic tilts.

Machine exercise: **Lower back extension**

Prone back raise

Lie face down on floor with arms and legs extended. Slowly lift
arms and upper trunk a few inches from floor. Pause a second
and return. Exhale up, inhale down.

Lower back extension

Cushion should be adjusted so you bend easily from waist with feet flat on platform. Cross arms and slowly stand erect. Return. Exhale up, inhale down.

4. Abdomen: Rectus abdominus (Abs)

Body weight exercise: **Crunches.** See also hanging-knee raises, pelvic tilts and diagonal crunches (latter for obliques).

Machine exercise: **Ab curl**

Crunches

Lie with knees bent and feet flat on floor. Place hands behind ears with elbows back out of sight. Slowly curl upper body toward ceiling. Keep lower back against floor. Pause a second and return. Exhale up, inhale down.

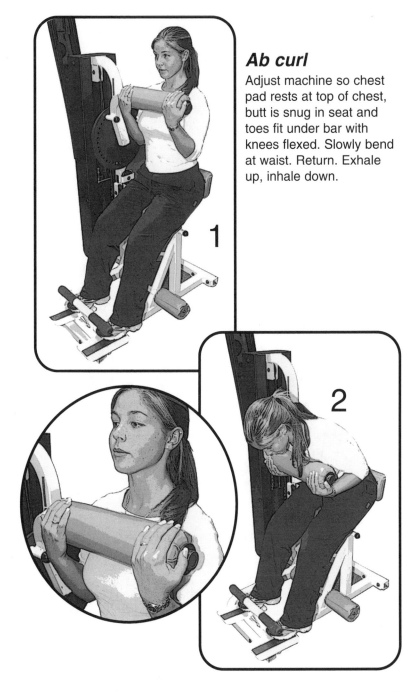

Ab curl

Adjust machine so chest pad rests at top of chest, butt is snug in seat and toes fit under bar with knees flexed. Slowly bend at waist. Return. Exhale up, inhale down.

5. Shoulders: Deltoids (Delts)

Body weight exercise: **Bar dips.** See also push-ups.

Free weight exercise: **Overhead press** with dumbbells. See also overhead press with barbell, upright rows, lateral raises, chest press, incline chest press, chest fly and incline chest fly.

Machine exercise: **Overhead press.** See also chest press and chest fly.

Bar dips

Grip bars and lower body until upper arms are parallel to floor. Body hangs straight down. Feet do not touch floor. Slowly push up* until arms are extended. Return. Exhale up, inhale down.

*If you cannot execute the exercise on your own, have someone provide push or use chair or bench.

Overhead press with dumbbells

Sit or stand erect. Hold dumbbells so that upper arms are parallel to floor, hands are over elbows and palms face forward. Lift dumbbells straight up with hands behind ears until elbows are fully extended. Return. Exhale up, inhale down.

1   2

1

Overhead press

Grasp handles with over-hand grip. Press bar until arms are extended straight up overhead. Lower arms to starting position. Exhale up, inhale down.

2

6. Upper arm/front: Biceps (Bi's)

Body weight exercise: **Chin-ups**

Free weight exercise: **Biceps curl** with dumbbells. See also biceps curl with barbells, bent-over one-arm rows and upright rows.

Machine exercise: **Biceps curl.** See also seated rows and front lat pulldowns.

Biceps curl with dumbbells

With a dumbbell in each hand, palms facing thighs, stand erect with feet hip-width apart and arms slightly bent. Slowly curl both dumbbells toward shoulders until palms face chest. Then lower arms to starting position. Exhale up, inhale down.

1   **2**

Biceps curl

Sit at machine placing the back of arms on pad. Seat should be adjusted to allow armpit to rest near top of the pad. Grasp bar with underhand grip. Raise handles until elbows are fully flexed. Upper arms stay on pad throughout. Lower handles until arms are fully extended. Exhale up, inhale down.

7. Upper arm/back: Triceps (Tri's)

Body weight exercise: **Push-ups** and bar dips.

Free weight exercise: **Triceps kickback.** See also triceps overhead extension, incline chest press and overhead press.

Machine exercise: **Triceps extension.** See also triceps pushdown, chest press and overhead press.

Triceps kickback

Hold dumbbell in one hand with palm facing side of body. Place other hand and knee on bench. Start with elbow bent at 90 degrees and slowly straighten arm backward until extended. Return to starting position. Only arm holding dumbbell should move. Exhale up, inhale down.

Triceps extension

Lie with knees up and feet flat on bench. Grasp cable bar and position directly over shoulders. Slowly flex arms at elbows until upper arms are parallel to floor. Upper arms should be perpendicular to floor throughout. Return.

Exhale up, inhale down.

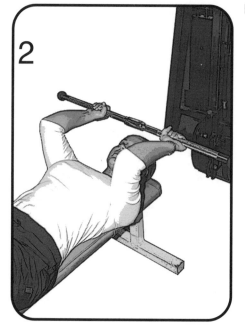

8. Upper leg/back: Gluteals (Glutes)

Body weight exercise: **Squats.** See also front, back and side lunges and step-ups.

Free weight exercise: **Step-ups** with dumbbells. See also step-ups with barbell, front and side lunges and squats.

Machine exercise: **Leg press**

1

2

Squats

Stand erect with feet hip-width apart. Slowly bend ankles, knees and hips until thighs are parallel to the floor. Keep back flat and head up. Knees do not extend beyond toes. Return to starting position. Exhale up, inhale down.

Step-ups with dumbbells

From erect standing position, lift one leg and place foot on bench that is about knee high. Lift body with leg and place other foot on bench. Slowly lower body by stepping back to starting position. Repeat with opposite leg. Exhale up, inhale down.

Leg press

Feet are shoulder-width apart, toes and knees facing straight ahead. With weight on heels, bend knees toward chest, keeping back flat and glutes and hips tight against back of machine. Once knees are close to chest, slowly straighten legs back to starting position. Exhale up, inhale down.

9. Thigh/front: Quadriceps (Quads)

Body weight exercise: **Front lunges.** See also back and side lunges, squats and step-ups.

Free weight exercise: **Squat** with dumbbells. See also squat with barbell, front and side lunges and step-ups.

Machine exercise: **Leg extension.** See also leg press.

Front lunges

From erect standing position, take a long step forward with first leg landing heel to toe. Lower body by flexing knee and hip of front leg until knee of rear leg is almost in contact with floor. Knee of forward leg should not extend past toes. Return to original standing position by forcibly extending the hip and knee of the forward leg. Repeat with opposite leg. Exhale up, inhale down.

Squat with dumbbells

With a dumbbell in each hand held palms in, stand erect with feet hip-width apart. Slowly bend ankles, knees and hips until thighs are parallel to the floor. Keep back flat and head up. Knees do not extend beyond toes. Return to starting position. Exhale up, inhale

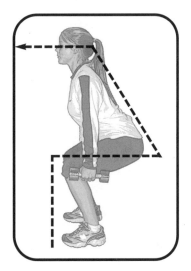

1

2

Leg extension

Sit with back against bench and top of ankles and feet under pad. Move pad forward by extending knees until legs are straight. Return pad to original position by bending knees. Exhale up, inhale down.

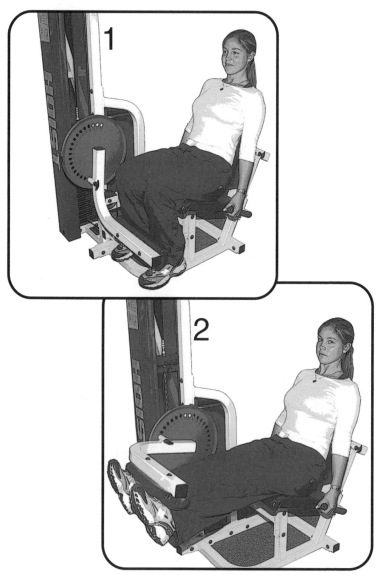

10. Thigh/back: Hamstrings (Hams)

Body weight exercise:	**Step-ups.** See also front, back and side lunges and squats.
Free weight exercise:	**Front lunge** with dumbbells. See also front lunge with barbell, side lunge, squats and step-ups.
Machine exercise:	**Leg curls.** See also leg press.

Step-ups

From erect standing position, place foot of first leg on bench. Stand on bench by extending the hip and knee of first leg and place foot of second leg on bench. Step down with second leg by flexing hip and knee of first leg. Return to original standing position and repeat with opposite leg. Exhale up, inhale down.

Front lunge with dumbbells

From erect standing position, take a long step forward with one leg. Bend knee and lower body until thigh is parallel to floor and knee is positioned directly over ankle. Other leg bends 90 degrees at knee. Step back to starting position and repeat with opposite leg. Exhale up, inhale down.

2   1

Leg curls

Lie face down on bench with lower legs under lever pad. Raise legs and lever pad to back of thighs by bending knees, keeping hips tight to bench. Lower legs and lever pad until knees are straight. Exhale up, inhale down.

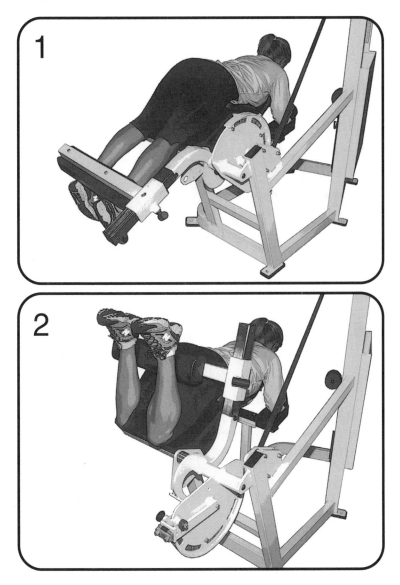

*Charting body part to
muscle to resistance type
to exercise (whew!)*

*Core muscle
exercise options*

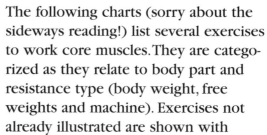

The following charts (sorry about the
sideways reading!) list several exercises
to work core muscles. They are catego-
rized as they relate to body part and
resistance type (body weight, free
weights and machine). Exercises not
already illustrated are shown with
instructions in the exer-
cise indexes: Chapters 9
through 9.3.

FTG 7.2 Core muscle exercise options

Ten major body parts, corresponding core muscles and exercise options for each

Upper Body, trunk

Body part	Muscle	Body weight	Free weights	Machines
1. Chest	Pectorals or Pecs	Push-ups: prone, incline, decline	Chest press Incline chest press *Chest fly *Incline chest fly	Chest press Chest fly
2. Upper back	Latissimus dorsi or Lats	Chin-ups	Pullovers *Bent-over one-arm rows	Front lat pulldowns Seated rows Seated pullovers
3. Lower back	Erector spinae	Prone back raise Pelvic tilts		Lower back extension
4. Midsection	Abdominal or Abs Obliques	Crunches Hanging-knee raises Pelvic tilts Diagonal crunches	* Dumbbell (DB) exercise only. All other free weight exercises may be performed with barbells (BB) or dumbbells.	Ab curl

Core muscle exercise options (continued)

Shoulders and arms

Body part	Muscle	Body weight	Free weights	Machines
5. Shoulders	Deltoids or Delts	Bar dips Push-ups: prone, incline, decline	Overhead press Upright rows *Lateral raises Chest press Incline chest press *Chest fly *Incline chest fly	Overhead press Chest press Chest fly
6. Upper arm/front	Biceps or Bi's	Chin-ups	Biceps curl *Bent-over one-arm rows Upright rows	Biceps curl Seated rows Front lat pulldowns
7. Upper arm/back	Triceps or Tri's	Push ups: prone, incline, decline Bar dips	*Triceps kickback Triceps overhead ext. Incline chest press Overhead press	Triceps extension Triceps pushdown Chest press Overhead press

Core muscle exercise options (continued)

Lower body

Body part	Muscle	Body weight	Free weights	Machines
8. Upper leg/back	Gluteals or Glutes	Squats Lunges: front, back, side Step-ups	Step-ups Squats Lunges: front and side	Leg press
9. Thigh/front	Quadriceps or Quads	Lunges: front, back, side Squats Step-ups	Squats Lunges: front and side Step-ups	Leg extension Leg press
10. Thigh/back	Hamstrings or Hams	Step-ups Lunges: front, back, side Squats	Lunges: front and side Squats Step-ups	Leg curls Leg press

FTG **7**.3 | *Suggested conditioning programs for beginning, intermediate and advanced strength training*

Recommended core conditioning programs

The programs outlined in the next two charts are specific regarding exercises, sets, reps and sessions. The first chart lays out a program using mostly free weights and the second a program using mostly machines. Each chart represents an extensive strength conditioning program. They are interchangeable. You don't do both during the same session!

Advancement
Advancement to a higher level requires more sets, less reps with greater weight (for free weight and machine exercises) and more sessions per week.

Start safely and conservatively
Beginners should note that it is safer to lift less weight and wise to limit sets and sessions until muscles grow stronger and technique improves.

Rep range

Remember that the weight you should lift is determined by the rep range rule.

Example:

DB squats require 12–15 reps in the beginning stage. The right weight for you will be manageable at 12 reps, increasingly difficult at 13 and 14 reps and barely possible to lift with good form at 15. It will be impossible for you to lift the weight properly 16 times.

Take the time to determine the weight you should lift. Advancing two levels of weight is significant improvement and should take place in 6–8 weeks of dedicated training.

10 core body parts / muscles

Body part	Muscle name proper / common
1. Chest	Pectoralis major (Pecs)
2. Upper back	Latissimus dorsi (Lats)
3. Lower back	Erector spinae
4. Abdomen	Rectus abdominus (Abs)
5. Shoulders	Deltoids (Delts)
6. Upper arm, front	Biceps (Bi's)
7. Upper arm, back	Triceps (Tri's)
8. Upper leg, back	Gluteus medius/maximus (Glutes)
9. Thigh, front	Quadriceps (Quads)
10. Thigh, back	Hamstrings (Hams)

Parts / muscles / abbreviations — Muscles in the charts are abbreviated. Once again, here are the 10 core body parts, corresponding core muscles and the abbreviated name for each. *Also used in the chart are:*
DB — Dumbbell
BB — Barbell
*Traps — Abbreviation for trapezius (upper back muscle)
** AMAP — As many as possible

Core conditioning: Free weights

General conditioning using free weight and body weight exercises
Suggested 6–8 week programs

Exercise	Muscles	Sets	Reps	X wk
Beginning				
DB squat	Quads / hams / glutes	1	12-15	2
DB chest press	Pecs / front delts / triceps	1	12-15	2
DB one-arm row	Lats / rear delts / biceps	1	12-15	2
DB overhead press	Delts / triceps	1	12-15	2
DB biceps curl	Biceps	1	12-15	2
DB triceps kickbks	Triceps	1	12-15	2
Crunches	Abs	1	20-25	2
Prone back raise	Erector spinae	1	12-15	2
Intermediate				
BB squat	Quads / hams / glutes	1-2	10-12	2-3
DB step-up	Quads / hams / glutes	1-2	10-12	2-3
BB chest press	Pecs / front delts / triceps	1-2	10-12	2-3
DB one-arm row	Lats / rear delts / biceps	1-2	10-12	2-3
DB incline press	Upper pecs / delts / tri's	1-2	10-12	2-3
BB biceps curls	Biceps	1-2	10-12	2-3
DB triceps overhd ext	Triceps	1-2	10-12	2-3
DB upright rows	Upper traps*	1-2	10-12	2-3
Pelvic tilts	Abs	1-2	20-25	2-3
Prone back raise	Erector spinae	1-2	12-15	2-3
Advanced				
BB squats	Quads / hams / glutes	2-3	6-10	2-3
DB lunges	Quads / hams / glutes	2-3	6-10	2-3
DB chest press	Pecs / front delts / triceps	2-3	6-10	2-3
BB incline press	Upper pecs / delts / tri's	2-3	6-10	2-3
Pull-ups	Lats / rear delts / biceps	2-3	AMAP**	2-3
DB one-arm row	Lats / rear delts / biceps	2-3	6-10	2-3
DB incline curls	Biceps	2-3	6-10	2-3
BB overhead ext	Triceps	2-3	6-10	2-3
DB upright rows	Delts / upper traps*	2-3	6-10	2-3
Dips	Pecs / front delts / triceps	2-3	6-10	2-3
Prone back raise	Erector spinae	2-3	12-15	2-3
Crunches	Abs	2-3	20-25	2-3

Core conditioning: Machines

General conditioning using machines and body weight exercises
Suggested 6–8 week programs

Exercise	Muscles	Sets	Reps	X wk
Beginning				
Leg press	Quads / hams / glutes	1	12-15	1
Chest press	Pecs / front delts / triceps	1	12-15	1
Seated row	Lats /rear delts / biceps	1	12-15	1
Overhead press	Delts / triceps	1	12-15	1
Pull-ups	Lats / rear delts / biceps	1	12-15	1
Dips	Pecs / front delts / triceps	1	12-15	1
Lower back extension	Erector spinae	1	12-15	1
Ab curls	Abs	1	20-25	1
Intermediate				
Leg press	Quads / hams / glutes	1-2	10-12	2-3
Leg extension	Quads	1-2	10-12	2-3
Leg curls	Hamstrings	1-2	10-12	2-3
Chest press	Pecs / front delts / triceps	1-2	10-12	2-3
Seated row	Lats / rear delts / biceps	1-2	10-12	2-3
Overhead press	Delts / triceps	1-2	10-12	2-3
Pull-ups	Lats / rear delts / biceps	1-2	10-12	2-3
Dips	Pecs / front delts / triceps	1-2	10-12	2-3
Back extensions	Erector spinae	1-2	10-12	2-3
Crunches	Abs	1-2	15-20	2-3
Advanced				
Leg press	Quads / hams / glutes	2-3	8-10	2-3
Leg extension	Quads	2-3	8-10	2-3
Leg curls	Hams	2-3	8-10	2-3
Hip ad– / abductions	Inner / outer thigh	2-3	8-10	2-3
Chest press	Pecs / front delts / tri's	2-3	8-10	2-3
Seated row	Lats / rear delts / biceps	2-3	8-10	2-3
Overhead press	Delts / triceps	2-3	8-10	2-3
Triceps extensions	Triceps	2-3	8-10	2-3
Pull-ups	Lats / rear delts / biceps	2-3	8-10	2-3
Dips	Pecs / front delts / tri's	2-3	8-10	2-3
Back extensions	Erector spinae	2-3	8-10	2-3
Crunches	Abs	2-3	15-20	2-3

Sport-specific strength training

Build a foundation first

Before attempting a sport-specific strength training program you should complete a core muscle development program presented earlier in this book. Young athletes need to develop balance and strength in all the major muscle groups before singling out particular muscles.

If you jump directly into a sport-specific program you are more likely to experience overuse injuries with the muscle or muscle group you are developing. Other undertrained muscles will be more prone to traumatic injuries as well — A chain is only as strong as its weakest link.

How long?

Like the core muscle program, we suggest you stay with a given sport-specific program from 6–8 weeks. However, you may safely attempt a more challenging workout program any time after you have advanced 2 weight levels with each exercise.

Power sports:
Gymnastics
Track and field
Girls who participate in gymnastics and track and field should be well prepared for success by following the core muscle program set forth earlier.

However, the exercises outlined in this chapter will definitely enhance performance.

These "power" sports use leg, chest and arm muscles in a pushing action. In gymnastics, leg power is essential for floor exercise, vaulting and balance beam. Grip strength is essential for the high bar, parallel bars and uneven bars. Sprinters, jumpers and throwers all need powerful leg muscles. Throwers and pole-vaulters require upper-body strength — especially in the pushing muscles of the chest, shoulders and triceps. All track and field athletes need strong midsections to transfer force from legs to the upper body. Total body lifts are a great way to knit all these muscles together.

Jumping sports:
Basketball
Figure skating
Volleyball
Basketball, figure skating and volley-ball require vertical jumping ability. Single-leg and double-leg take-offs are powered by the lower body. Shoulder muscles also help the jumping action by producing a powerful upward thrust.

Proper performance of the exercises listed will strengthen jumping muscles and should improve jumping quality and quantity. Young athletes should be able to jump higher and perform successive jumps with less loss of power.

Special note:
Although it may appear to be a logical training method, never try to imitate actual jumping movements with heavy weights. This is difficult and dangerous.

Striking sports:
Field hockey
 Golf
 Softball
 Tennis
The sports of field hockey, golf, softball and tennis have many differences, mostly related to movement patterns. Softball requires sprinting ability to run the bases, tennis requires more lateral movement and golf requires a very specific swinging ability. Field hockey combines a little of each.

However, all these sports share one very important component: striking a ball. Even though the horizontal swinging action of softball and tennis is different from the vertical swinging action of field hockey and golf, the mechanics of developing striking force are the same. In horizontal and vertical striking movements, power comes from the large muscles of the legs and hips via a powerful thrust that transfers weight from the back leg to the front leg. The torquing action of the midsection, whether horizontal or diagonal, transfers power from the lower body to the upper body.

Perform the suggested exercises with slow to moderate speed through a full range of motion. This maximizes muscle involvement and minimizes any impact or help from momentum.

Endurance sports:

Soccer
Cross country
Distance running
Swimming
Athletes who participate in soccer, cross country, distance running and swimming are constantly in action. Therefore, a high level of cardiovascular and muscle endurance is a must.

Although these aerobic activities are less dependent on muscle strength than other sports, strength training should play an important role in conditioning. Distance running and cross country utilize the same lower body muscles. Swimming relies heavily on upper body strength. Soccer requires lower body and neck strength.

As a rule, athletes in endurance activities respond better to high repetitions with low weight loads. We recommend you begin with 15-20 reps per set. As you grow stronger and progress to higher levels of weight, make sure reps are no less than 10-15 per set.

Also, due to emphasis on sustained muscle activity, athletes should perform sets of each exercise with only a short rest between sets, say 30 seconds to a minute.

About total body lifts

A simple definition of a total body lift is lifting a weight while standing. Lifting on your feet requires synergy and stability. Movements made during a total body lift are also the most common and fundamental in sports.

Proper, sustained total body lifting will:

1. Prevent injury.

2. Enhance your ability to "explode" (generate power quickly).

3. Teach you to apply force with muscle groups in the right sequence.

4. Enhance your ability to accelerate objects under varying degrees of resistance.

5. Measure your effectiveness in generating power to a greater degree than any other means of weight training.

Sport-specific development programs

Displayed to the right are 13 popular sports and specific exercises for each that will enhance performance. Most of the exercises are free weight exercises* and can be executed with dumbbells or a barbell. Stick with a program made up of the exercises marked under your sport for a period of 6–8 weeks or until you have advanced 2 weight levels in each exercise. See Chapters 9, 9.1 and 9.2 for illustrations and instructions of exercises not already presented in *Chapter 7.1: Core muscle strength training.*

*One-arm rows, lateral raises, triceps kickbacks and shoulder internal and external rotations require dumbbells only. Chin-ups, bar dips, prone back extension, crunches and diagonal crunches are body weight exercises. The power clean and the push press are total body lifts (see previous page).

New exercises (exercises not mentioned in the core group) are heel raises, incline biceps curls, shrugs, shoulder internal and external rotations, wrist curls, power cleans and push presses (below). See *Chapter 9.1: Free weight index* for illustrations and instructions.

Exercise	Works this body part / muscle
Heel raise	Lower leg / gastrocnemius / calves
Incline biceps curl	Upper arm / biceps or bi's
Shrugs	Upper back / neck / trapezius or traps
Internal rotation External rotation	Rotator cuff muscles (shoulder)
Wrist curl	Forearm / wrist flexors
Power clean	Total body
Push press	Total body

Sports

Exercises

Exercise	Basketball	Cross country	Distance running	Field hockey	Figure skating	Golf	Gymnastics	Soccer	Softball	Swimming	Tennis	Track & field	Volleyball
Squat	X	X	X	X	X	X	X	X	X	X	X	X	X
Step-up	X	X	X	X	X				X	X	X	X	X
Lunge	X			X	X		X		X	X	X	X	X
Side lunge	X			X	X	X	X	X			X		
Heel raise	X	X	X	X	X		X	X	X			X	X
Chest press		X	X	X	X	X		X				X	
Incline chest press	X						X		X	X	X	X	X
Pullover	X	X	X		X	X		X	X	X		X	X
One-arm row	X			X	X	X	X	X	X	X	X	X	
Lateral raise	X	X	X			X		X	X				
Overhead press	X	X		X	X		X			X	X	X	X
Biceps curl	X	X		X	X	X	X	X					
Incline biceps curl		X								X	X	X	X
Triceps kickback	X	X		X	X	X		X	X	X	X		
Triceps overhd ext		X		X		X		X				X	X
Chin-ups		X	X	X		X	X		X	X		X	X
Bar dips		X	X	X		X	X			X		X	X
Prone back ext	X	X	X	X	X	X	X	X	X	X	X	X	X
Crunches		X	X	X		X		X	X				
Diagonal crunches	X	X		X	X	X	X	X	X		X	X	X
Hanging-knee raises	X	X	X	X	X	X	X	X	X	X		X	X
Shrugs		X	X	X			X		X			X	
Shoulder rotations			X							X	X	X	X
Wrist curl	X			X	X	X	X	X	X		X	X	
Power clean			X		X	X		X		X		X	X
Push press	X				X			X					

Medicine ball exercises

A medicine ball is a weighted ball and is especially effective in exercising muscles and surrounding tissues with true sport motion.

Perform the exercises listed below the sport category of your choice. Do these exercises in place of those in the grid for a change of pace. Medicine ball exercises are listed and illustrated with instructions in *Chapter 9.3: Medicine ball index.*

Determine the weight of the ball you should use for each exercise the same way you determine weight for free weight and machine exercising *(see Chapter 7: Repetition range rule).*

Like total body lifts, movements required to execute medicine ball exercises closely match those movements needed in sports.

Medicine ball exercises

Exercise	Area worked
Power Sports	
Squat toss	Legs, chest, arms
Lunge pass	Legs, chest, arms
Underhand throw	Legs, shoulders, trunk, arms
Side pass	Trunk, arms
Trunk rotations	Abdominal, obliques
Jumping Sports	
Squat jump	Legs, shoulders, arms
Squat toss	Legs, chest, arms
Side pass	Trunk, arms
Striking Sports	
Squat toss	Legs, chest, arms
Lunge pass	Legs, chest, arms
Underhand throw	Legs, shoulders, trunk, arms
Trunk rotations	Abdominal, obliques
Single-arm throw	Trunk, rotator cuff
Endurance Sports	
Squat toss	Legs, chest, arms
Lunge pass	Legs, chest, arms
Side pass	Trunk, arms

Use exercises from this chart to complement those from the sports-specific grid.

Medicine ball exercises are listed and illustrated with instructions in *Chapter 9.3: Medicine ball index.*

Body weight index

Exercises displayed in this section are those listed but not illustrated in Chapters 7.1—7.3 and 8.

Incline push-ups
Decline push-ups
Pelvic tilts
Diagonal crunches
Hanging-knee raises
Back lunges
Side lunges

Incline push-ups

Parts (muscles) worked:
Chest (pecs), shoulders (delts) and
upper arms (triceps).

Decline push-ups

An incline push-up is performed with hands elevated, toes on the floor.

A decline push-up is performed with feet elevated, hands on the floor.

Lie face down and position hands in line with chest. With legs and body straight, push up until arms are extended. Lower body without chest touching. Return. Exhale up, inhale down.

Pelvic tilts

Lie on floor with knees bent and feet, hands and arms flat on floor. Slowly lift hips as far as you can. Pause a second and return. Exhale up, inhale down.

Parts (muscles) worked:
Lower back (erector spinae).

Diagonal crunches

1

2

Lie on floor with knees bent and feet flat on floor. Place hands behind ears with elbows back out of sight. Slowly curl one arm toward opposite knee. Keep lower back against floor. Pause a second and return. Exhale up, inhale down.

Parts (muscles) worked:
Midsection (obliques).

Hanging-knee raises

Grasp bar palms out and hang with body straight and fully extended. Slowly lift knees to chest. Pause a second and return. Do not rock. Exhale up, inhale down.

Parts (muscles) worked:
Midsection (abs).

Back lunges

From erect standing position, take large step back landing on forefoot. Lower body by flexing knee and hip of front leg until knee of rear leg is almost in contact with floor. Repeat with opposite leg. Exhale up, inhale down.

Parts (muscles) worked:
Upper leg back (glutes), thigh front (quads) and thigh back (hams).

Side lunges

From erect standing position, take a large step to side with first leg. Lower body by flexing at knee and hip. Lunging foot faces forward with shoulders pulled back and chest up. Return by pushing off bent leg, keeping upper body straight. Repeat with opposite leg. Exhale up, inhale down.

Parts (muscles) worked:
Upper leg back (glutes), thigh front (quads) and thigh back (hams).

Free weight index

Exercises displayed in this section are those listed but not illustrated in Chapters 7.1–7.3 and 8.

DB — Dumbbell
BB — Barbell

Chest press BB
Incline chest press DB/BB
Chest fly
Incline chest fly
Bent-over one-arm rows
Pullovers BB
Upright rows DB
Overhead press BB
Lateral raise DB
Biceps curl BB
Triceps overhead
  extension DB/BB
Squats BB
Front lunges BB
Side lunges DB
Step-ups BB

Additional free weight exercises for sport-specific muscle development:

Heel raises DB/BB
Incline biceps curl DB
Shrugs DB
Shoulder internal rotation
Shoulder external rotation
Wrist curl DB

Total body lifts:
Power clean BB
Push press BB

Chest press with barbell

Lie with knees up, feet flat on bench and arms extended
straight up. Slowly bend elbows and lower weight to chest
without touching. Press up until arms are fully extended. Head,
shoulders and buttocks in contact with bench at all times.
Hands positioned over elbows at all times. Exhale up, inhale

1

2

Parts (muscles) worked:
Chest (pecs) and shoulders (delts).

Incline chest press with dumbbells

Lie on incline bench with feet flat on floor. Extend arms and weights straight up. Dumbbells are held at right angles to torso and bench. Slowly bend elbows and lower weights until upper arms are parallel to floor. Press up until arms are fully extended. Head, shoulders and buttocks in contact with bench at all times. Hands positioned over elbows at all times. Exhale up, inhale down.

1

2

Parts (muscles) worked:
Chest (pecs), shoulders (delts) and upper arms (triceps).

Incline chest press with barbell

Lie on incline bench with feet flat on floor. Extend arms and weight straight up. Slowly bend elbows and lower weight to chest without touching. Press up until arms are fully extended. Head, shoulders and buttocks in contact with bench at all times. Hands positioned over elbows at all times.

Exhale up, inhale down.

1

2

Parts (muscles) worked:
Chest (pecs), shoulders (delts) and upper arms (triceps).

Chest fly

Lie with knees up, feet flat on bench and arms extended straight up. Dumbbells are held parallel to torso and bench. Slowly bend elbows and lower weights until upper arms are parallel to floor. Press up until arms are fully extended. Head, shoulders and buttocks in contact with bench at all times. Hands positioned over elbows at all times. Exhale up, inhale down.

1

2

Parts (muscles) worked:
Chest (pecs) and shoulders (delts).

Incline chest fly

Lie on incline bench with feet flat on floor. Extend arms and weights straight up. Dumbbells are held parallel to torso and bench. Slowly bend elbows and lower weights until upper arms are parallel to floor. Press up until arms are fully extended. Head, shoulders and buttocks in contact with bench at all times. Hands positioned over elbows at all times. Exhale up, inhale down.

1

2

Parts (muscles) worked:
Chest (pecs) and shoulders (delts).

Bent-over one-arm rows

Bend over and place knee and flat of hand on bench. Back is parallel to floor. Fully extend opposite arm with weight toward floor. Slowly pull dumbbell until it reaches side of chest. Then lower dumbbell back to straight arm position. Back should not rotate during this exercise. Exhale up, inhale down.

1

2

Parts (muscles) worked:
Upper back (lats) and biceps.

Pullovers with barbell

Lie on bench with knees up, feet flat and arms extended straight up. Slowly lower barbell over your head with arms straight until arms are parallel to ground. Return. Exhale up,

Parts (muscles) worked:
Upper back (lats).

Upright rows with dumbbells

Stand erect with arms extended down and dumbbells held evenly in front. Slowly raise weights to collarbone. Lower arms until once again extended. Exhale up, inhale down.

1   **2**

Parts (muscles) worked:
Shoulders (delts) and upper arm (biceps).

Overhead press with barbell

Sit or stand erect. Hold barbell at chin level (not resting on chest). Hands over elbows and palms face forward. Lift barbell straight up until elbows are fully extended. Return. Exhale up, inhale down.

1

2

Parts (muscles) worked:
Shoulders (delts) and upper arm (triceps).

Lateral raise

1

Sit or stand erect with arms extended down at sides and palms facing thighs. Slowly lift both dumbbells sideward until arms are parallel to floor. Keep arms slightly bent. Return to starting position. Exhale up, inhale down.

2

Parts (muscles) worked:
Shoulders (delts).

Biceps curl with barbell

Stand erect with feet hip-width apart, arms slightly bent and palms facing forward. Slowly curl barbell toward shoulders until palms face chest. Lower arms to starting position. Exhale up, inhale down.

Parts (muscles) worked:
Upper arm (biceps).

Triceps over-head extension with dumbbells

Lie on bench with knees up and feet flat. Extend weights straight up. Hold dumbbells parallel to torso and bench. Slowly lower weights over your head until upper arms have traveled 90 degrees. Keep upper arms perpendicular to the floor throughout. Pause briefly, then return. Exhale up, inhale down.

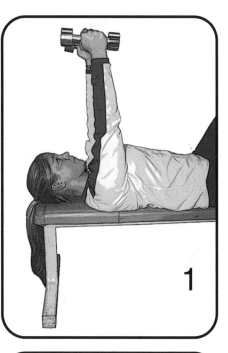

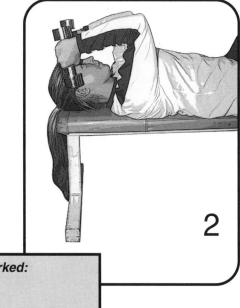

Parts (muscles) worked:
Upper arm (triceps).

Triceps overhead extension with barbell

Lie on bench with knees up and feet flat. Extend weight straight up. Slowly lower weight over your head until upper arms have traveled 90 degrees. Keep upper arms perpendicular to the floor throughout. Pause briefly, then return. Exhale up, inhale down.

1

2

Parts (muscles) worked:
Upper arm (triceps).

Squats with barbell

Stand erect with feet hip-width apart. Barbell is held across shoulders, behind neck, palms forward. Slowly bend ankles, knees and hips until thighs are parallel to the floor. Keep back flat and head up. Knees do not extend beyond toes. Return to starting position. Exhale up, inhale down.

Parts (muscles) worked:
Upper leg/back (glutes), thigh front (quads) and thigh back (hams).

Front lunge with barbell

Stand erect with feet hip-width apart.
Barbell is held across shoulders,
behind neck, palms forward. Take a
long step forward with right leg.
Bend knee and lower body until right
thigh is parallel to floor and right
knee is positioned directly over
ankle of right foot. Meanwhile bend
left leg so it is 90 degrees at knee.
Step back to starting position and
repeat with other leg. Exhale up,
inhale down.

1

2

Parts (muscles) worked:
Upper leg/back (glutes), thigh front
(quads) and thigh back (hams).

Side lunge with dumbbells

From erect standing position, lunge to side with one leg. Point toe slightly in direction of lunge. Bend knee until thigh is parallel to floor. Push back to starting position. Repeat with opposite leg. Keep entire body square throughout. Exhale up, inhale down.

Parts (muscles) worked:
Upper leg/back (glutes), thigh front (quads), thigh back (hams), inner and outer thigh (abductors and adductors).

Step-ups with barbell

Stand erect with barbell resting on shoulders back of neck. Step onto a bench that is about knee high. Lift body with that leg and place foot alongside first foot. Slowly lower body by stepping back to starting position. Repeat with opposite leg. Exhale up, inhale down.

Parts (muscles) worked:
Upper leg/back (glutes), thigh front (quads) and hip flexors.

FTG **9**.1.1

Additional free weight exercises for sport-specific development

DB — Dumbbell
BB — Barbell

Heel raises DB/BB
Incline biceps curl DB
Shrugs DB
Shoulder external rotation
Shoulder internal rotation
Wrist curl DB

Total body lifts:
Power clean BB
Push press BB

Heel raises with dumbbells

Stand erect and raise up on toe or toes as high as possible. Then slowly lower heel. Exhale up, inhale down. Try this without step or block first.

Parts (muscles) worked:
Lower leg/calf (tibialis anterior).

Heel raises with barbell

Same instructions as previous page. Barbell rests on shoulders and upper back (traps).

Incline biceps curl with dumbbells

Lie on incline bench with feet flat on floor. Arms extend down and dumbbells are held palms facing body and bench. Slowly curl and rotate dumbbells toward shoulders until palms face chest. Lower arms to starting position. Exhale up, inhale down.

1

2

Parts (muscles) worked:
Upper arms (biceps).

Shrugs with dumbbells

Stand erect with arms extending down. Hands hold dumbbells palms facing body. Slowly shrug shoulders up, front to back and down in a circular motion. Exhale up, inhale down.

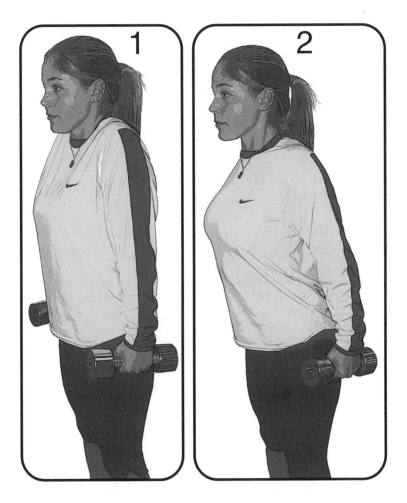

Parts (muscles) worked:
Upper back and neck (trapezius or traps).

Shoulder external rotation

Lie on side, rest on elbow. Other arm grasps dumbbell palm down with elbow resting on hip. Slowly rotate weight up until lower arm is at right angle to floor. Return. Repeat with other arm. Exhale up, inhale down.

Parts (muscles) worked:
Rotator cuff musculature.

Shoulder internal rotation

Lie on back with knees up, feet flat and upper arms in contact with floor. Hold dumbbells straight up, palms in.
Keeping the 90 degree angle of elbow joint, slowly lower weights to floor, pause and return. Exhale up, inhale down.

1

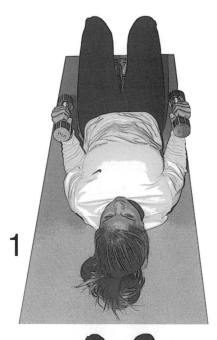

2

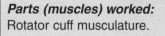

Parts (muscles) worked:
Rotator cuff musculature.

Wrist curls with dumbbells / wrist flexors

Sit erect and hold dumbbells with palms facing up and slightly forward. Slowly flex the fingers and wrists as high as possible until palms face body. Keep forearms flat against thighs or bench and parallel to floor throughout. Return. Exhale up, inhale down.

1

2

Parts (muscles) worked:
Wrists and forearms (wrist flexors).

Wrist curls with dumbbells / wrist extenders

Sit erect and hold dumbbells with palms facing floor. Slowly lift fingers and wrists as high as possible while keeping forearms flat on thighs or bench and parallel to floor. Return. Exhale up, inhale down.

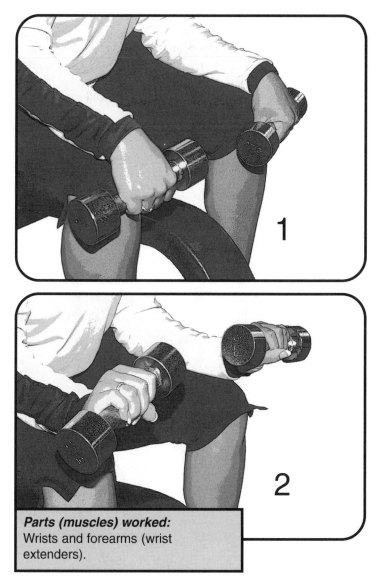

Parts (muscles) worked:
Wrists and forearms (wrist extenders).

Total body lift:
Power clean with barbell

1. Feet shoulder width, toes straight, knees over bar.

2. Grip bar just outside knees.

3. Lift bar smoothly (don't jerk) to just below knees using legs. Knees, hips and shoulders move upward together. Bar moves at rate of hip. Keep shoulders above hips.

4. Keep bar close to body and move bar in straight line from floor.

5. Shrug and lift elbows high to ears. Straighten legs. Stand on toes.

6. Explode hips inward (roll).

7. Head is up (don't dip head before clean or before lift from floor).

8. Spread feet and re-bend knee at catch phase.

9. Clean weight by throwing elbows forward.

10. Set weight on floor by bending at knees and hips (don't bend at back).

Total body lift: Push press with barbell

Same as barbell squat initially. As you begin to lift, transfer energy from push off ground through your body and accelerate upward. Lift arms as legs straighten and continue lift until arms are locked above head with hands behind ears. Exhale up, inhale down.

1

2

3

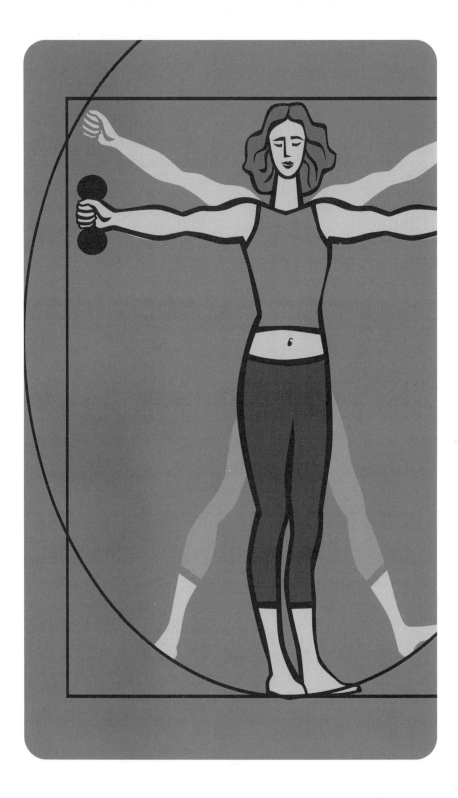

Machine index

*Exercises displayed in this
section are those listed
but not illustrated in
Chapters 7.1-7.3.*

Hip abduction
Hip adduction
Chest fly
Seated rows
Triceps pushdown

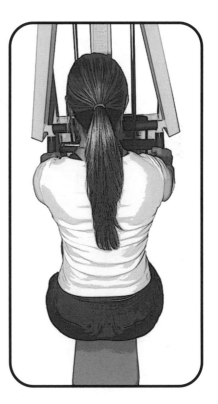

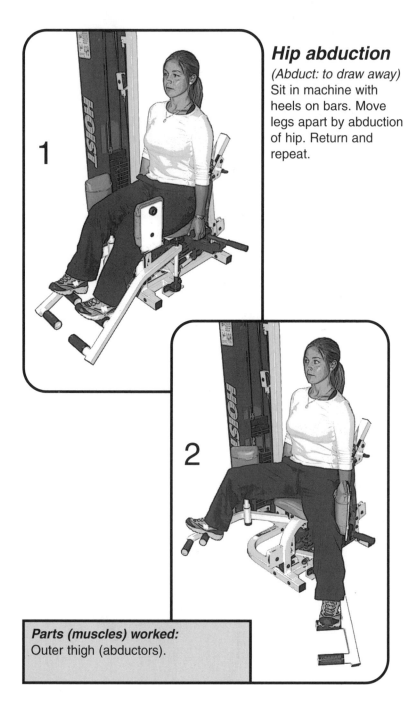

Hip abduction

(Abduct: to draw away)
Sit in machine with heels on bars. Move legs apart by abduction of hip. Return and repeat.

1

2

Parts (muscles) worked:
Outer thigh (abductors).

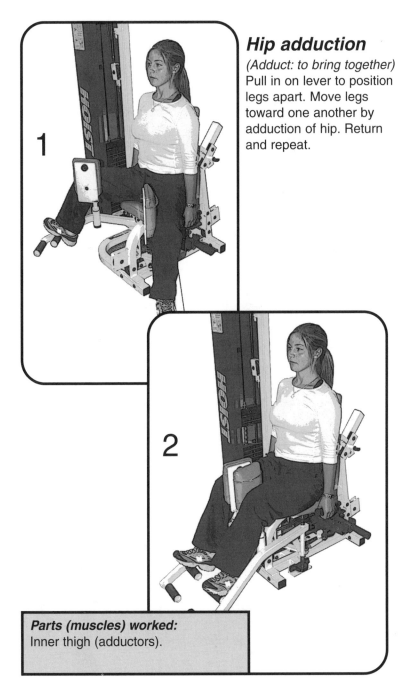

Hip adduction

(Adduct: to bring together)
Pull in on lever to position legs apart. Move legs toward one another by adduction of hip. Return and repeat.

Parts (muscles) worked:
Inner thigh (adductors).

Chest fly

Sit with back against machine and forearms on arm pads. Push arms together keeping chest up. Return arms to starting position until chest muscles are stretched. Exhale as arms come together, inhale as arms go back out.

Parts (muscles) worked:
Chest (pecs) and shoulders (delts).

Seated rows

Sit with chest against pad. Use an overhand grip on handles. Pull handles back until elbows are behind back, shoulders are pulled back and shoulder blades are squeezed together. Return until arms are extended. Exhale as arms go back and inhale as arms extend forward.

1

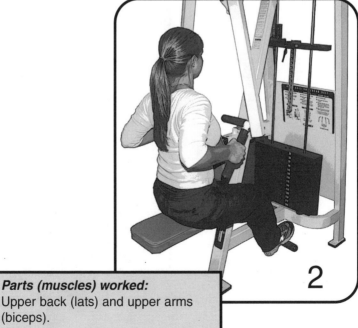

2

Parts (muscles) worked:
Upper back (lats) and upper arms (biceps).

Triceps pushdowns

Grasp cable bars with overhand grip. Position elbows to sides. Extend arms straight down. Return bar until forearms are close to upper arm. Exhale down, inhale up.

Parts (muscles) worked:
Upper arms (triceps).

Medicine ball index

*Exercises displayed in this
section are those listed
but not illustrated in
Chapter 8.*

Squat toss
Lunge pass
Underhand throw
Side pass
Trunk rotations
Squat jump
Single-arm throw

Squat toss

Hold ball directly in front of chest with feet shoulder-width apart. Slowly bend knees and hips until thighs are parallel to floor. Keep back flat, head up and eyes straight ahead. Quickly jump and toss ball as high as possible in front of you. Exhale up, inhale down.

Lunge pass

Hold ball directly in front of chest with feet hip-width apart. Take long step forward and quickly push ball off chest as you bend legs. Exhale during push, inhale once ball is gone and exhale back to starting position.

Underhand throw

Hold ball in squat position with arms straight and ball close to floor. Come up sharply from squat and throw ball as high as possible. Exhale up, inhale down.

Side pass

Begin with ball just below chest.
Swing ball across body and
pass it toward partner. Pivot
back foot as ball is transferred
across body. Switch sides after
completing desired number of
reps. Exhale as you throw,
inhale as you wind up.

1

2

Trunk rotations

Assume an erect sitting position and place ball behind you. Rotate trunk to one side, pick up ball with both hands, bring it across body and place it behind you. Exhale when ball is in hand, inhale on return without ball. Switch sides after completing desired number of reps.

4

3

2

1

Squat jump

Same as squat toss except ball
remains in hands in front of
chest during jump. Exhale up,
inhale down.

Single-arm throw

Stand with one foot in front of the other. Hold ball in one hand at ear level. Step forward and throw ball with standard (over-the-ear) throwing motion. Repeat with other arm. Exhale on throw, inhale during wind up.

3

3

Eating

*Keeping it simple:
What to eat and drink
in pursuit of health and
physical development*

The amount of information regarding nutrition is over-whelming. The problem with so much information is that it can be conflicting, confusing and complicated — so complicated that nothing sticks.

What to eat — at least read this!

1. Eat lots of whole grain foods.
2. Eat lots of dark-green leafy vegetables and deeply colored fruits.
3. Eat and drink lots of low-fat milk products.
4. Eat lean meats, more fish, beans and nuts.
5. Easy on sugar added foods.

Although what makes our bodies work is complex, what it needs — for energy, to build strong bones and muscles and to otherwise be healthy — is not.

Food Guide Pyramid

Chances are you have seen the Food Guide Pyramid. It's fairly conspicuous — on the labels and packages of certain food items, especially whole grain products. You need not look much further to understand good eating habits.

The Food Guide Pyramid was developed by the United States Department of Agriculture and the United States Department of Health and Human Services to illustrate simply and specifically what healthy eating is.

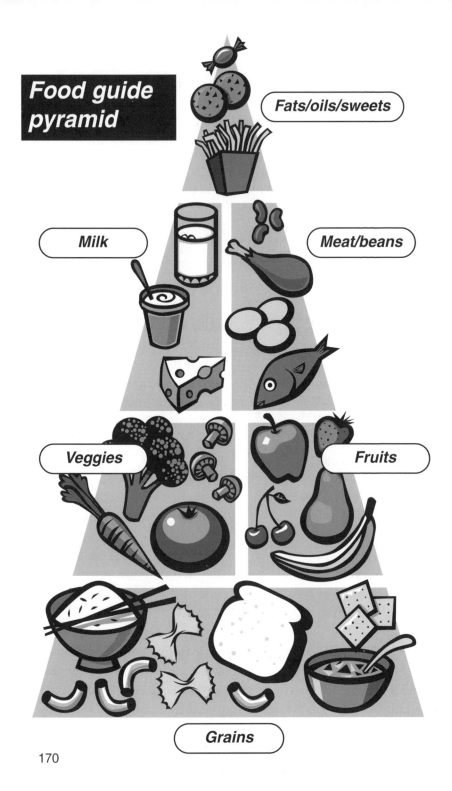

Food guide pyramid

Fats/oils/sweets

Milk

Meat/beans

Veggies

Fruits

Grains

The pyramid encourages variety, balance and moderation in daily food choices. By and large, if you adhere to its guidelines you will satisfy your nutritional needs. Of course, as you train harder you may need to eat more calories to meet higher energy demands. However, the general principals of the pyramid still hold.

By developing healthy eating habits now you can promote your health for a lifetime. You will minimize your risk for chronic diseases such as heart disease, some types of cancer, stroke, diabetes and osteoporosis (brittleness and porosity of the bones, resulting in a higher likelihood of fracture). A nutritious diet can also lessen major risk factors for chronic disease such as high blood pressure, obesity and high blood cholesterol.

Represented in the Pyramid are the five major food groups:

(1) Grains Group
The base of the Pyramid consists of the Grains Group of foods. Included in this block are bread, cereal, rice and pasta. It's the largest block in the Pyramid and the supporting one. It's important to eat most of your food from this group.

Eat whole grains
Whole grains contain vitamins, minerals, fiber and other protective substances that promote health. It should be noted that there is a substantial nutritional difference between refined grains and whole grains. Refined grains are low in fiber. Fiber is important because it

helps bowels function properly. It's also important to eat a variety of whole grains because different grains differ in nutritional value.

(2) Fruit Group and (3) Vegetable Group

Above the Grains Group are the Fruit and Vegetable Groups. These are the next largest blocks and they should comprise the next largest part of your diet.

Eat dark-green leafy vegetables and deeply colored fruits

Fruits and vegetables contain fiber, vitamins, minerals and other nutrients important for optimum health. Especially rich in nutritional value are dark-green leafy vegetables, deeply colored fruits, dry beans and peas. Try to eat a variety of colors and kinds to maximize your intake of nutrients.

(4) Milk Group and (5) Meat and Beans Group

The Milk Group is a major source of calcium and other nutrients. The idea here is to decrease fat intake, especially saturated fats which tend to raise blood cholesterol and increase the risk of coronary heart disease. Eating too much fat of any type can yield excess calories. Fat-free or low-fat milk and yogurt and low-fat cheese are wise choices.

> **No need to be a food scrooge!**
> *Eating right is not about deprivation. It's about making better food choices on a regular basis. If you eat nourishing foods most of the time and follow a serious exercise program you can have that occasional pizza or ice cream cone — no problem!*

Eat lean meats, more fish, beans and nuts

Meats, fish and beans are your protein sources. Again, avoid fat. Select lean meats and trim off any fat. Take the skin off poultry. Eat more fish. Eat dry beans, peas and lentils. Limit your intake of high-fat processed meats such as bacon, sausages, salami and bologna as well as liver and other organ meats.

Better to avoid fats, oils and sweets

At the top of the Pyramid is the smallest block and the types of food you should eat less frequently — fats, oils and sweets. Make no mistake, the body needs a certain amount of fat. Among other things, you need fat to absorb certain types of vitamins. However, in most teen diets there is seldom insufficient fat. Better to limit your overall intake of fat — especially meat and dairy fats.

Sugars and starches appear naturally in many foods such as breads, cereals, grains, milk, fruits and certain vegetables that also supply other important nutrients. Avoid eating foods with added sugars, like soft drinks and candy. Taking in excess calories from these foods may result in lower consumption of more nutritious fare and weight gain (but see inset *No need to be a food scrooge!*).

Importance of drinking fluids

To prevent dehydration you must maintain fluid levels. Take frequent water breaks before, during and after physical activity. You should drink 4-8 ounces of fluid every 15-20 minutes of activity.

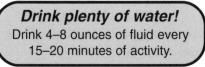

Drink plenty of water!
Drink 4–8 ounces of fluid every 15–20 minutes of activity.

It's important to remember that dehydration can be reached before feeling thirsty. Warning signs include fatigue, irritability and a sudden decline in performance (these are also symptoms of inadequate caloric intake).

Drink water when you train

Juice, carbonated and caffeinated beverages should not be used for fluid replacement during activity. Juice and soda may cause a number of stomach problems. Drinking caffeinated beverages results in frequent bathroom breaks and may cause agitation and headaches. Sports drinks are OK. Your best bet is water!

Training diet: carbos, protein and fats

A complete and balanced training diet for physical activity will provide 55% to 60% of total energy from carbohydrates (carbos, carbs), 12% to 15% from protein and 25% to 30% from fat. These proportions are supported by the Food Guide Pyramid.

High-carbo foods

Grains, breads and cereals
Oatmeal
Rice
Graham crackers
Flour tortilla
Spaghetti
Whole wheat bread
Fig bar
Popcorn
Cheerios
Shredded wheat
Waffle
Pretzels

Fruits
Banana
Cantaloupe
Dried apricot
Raisins
Orange
Cranberry juice
Orange juice
Apple
Peach
Pear

Vegetables
Carrots
Corn
Baked potato

Beans
Garbanzo beans
Pinto beans
Kidney beans
Navy beans

Dairy
Yogurt

The body prefers and gets most of its energy from carbohydrates. The main form in which carbohydrate is stored in the body is glycogen. The primary job of protein is the growth and repair of body tissue. Fats also supply energy and enable the body to absorb certain vitamins necessary for the body to maintain itself.

**Feeling run down?
Check carbo intake
and fluid levels**
If your usual exercise intensity becomes compromised, the cause is usually inadequate carbohydrate intake or dehydration. Sustaining a carbohydrate-rich diet and scheduling rest days to allow adequate muscle glycogen synthesis can prevent glycogen depletion. Remember to drink 4–8 ounces of water every 15–20 minutes of activity to prevent dehydration.

Improving glycogen storage and recovery time
You can increase muscle glycogen storage and improve recovery time by consuming

high-carbohydrate fluids and foods after training (within 30 minutes after activity and once again 2 hours later).

Eating before exercise
The pre-exercise meal prevents you from feeling hungry before or during workouts and supplies fuel to muscles during activity. Carbohydrate-rich food should be eaten any-where from 1–4 hours before exercise depending on the type of food (see inset).

> ### Pre-exercise meal guide
> **1 to 2 hours before exercise**
> • Fruit or vegetable juices
> • Fresh, low-fiber fruit
>
> **2 to 3 hours before exercise**
> • Fruit or vegetable juices
> • Fresh fruit
> • Breads, bagels, crackers
>
> **3 or more hours before exercise**
> • Fruit or vegetable juices
> • Fresh fruit
> • Breads, bagels, crackers
> • Peanut butter, lean meat, low-fat cheese
> • Low-fat yogurt
> • Pasta
> • Cereal with low-fat milk

Foods to avoid before exercise
Fatty foods — Because they are slow to digest and pro-duce a sluggish feeling. Fatty foods include many high-protein foods such as meat, cheese and eggs.

High-fiber foods — Because they can cause cramps and inopportune bathroom breaks (especially foods high in bran).

Beans, broccoli, cauliflower and onion — Because they cause gas.

Salty foods — Because they can cause a bloated feeling and fluid retention.

About alcohol

Adolescents should not drink alcoholic beverages. They provide no health benefit. Furthermore, research indicates the risk of abuse increases when consumption starts at an early age.

Vegetarian diets

A semi-vegetarian diet can obtain necessary calories and protein from eggs and dairy products. Although vegetable sources alone can provide adequate nourishment to foster physical development and hard workouts, it does take careful planning. It may be a challenge for girls to obtain sufficient protein, calories and other nutrients such as calcium, zinc, iron and vitamins D and B12 on a strict vegetarian diet.

Iron-rich foods

Turkey, beef, pork
Shrimp
Dried fruit
Kidney beans
Cream of wheat
Fortified cereal
Liver

Calcium-rich foods

Whole milk
Cottage cheese
Cheese
Yogurt
Canned salmon
Tofu
Broccoli
Eggs

Iron and calcium needs for girls

Active adolescent girls are at increased risk of iron deficiency for a number of reasons including exercise-related loss, inadequate dietary intake, low energy intake, increased growth demands and menstruation. Inadequate consumption may place you at risk for iron-deficiency anemia (a pathological deficiency in the oxygen-carrying material of blood) and a marked decline in performance.

It is reported that adolescents eat only one-half to two-thirds of the Recommended Daily Allowances (RDA) for calcium. Diets lacking calcium may place you at risk for stress fractures and osteoporosis.

For the most part, eating a regular diet of normal foods will supply enough iron and calcium. Problems arise when girls stop eating all meat and dairy products in order to make sure they avoid fats or because they are vegetarians. See inset that includes *Iron-rich* and *Calcium-rich foods.*

Supplements cannot replace ordinary food
Scientific evidence does not support the general use of supplements or vitamins to improve performance. Active girls must understand and be confident that a regular diet of nourishing, everyday food will promote muscle growth and optimal performance.

Comparing exercises with calories
Calories (kcl) burned every 10 minutes of activity

Your weight in pounds*	75	90	100	110	120	130	145
Basketball	60	68	77	85	94	102	110
Calisthenics	23	26	30	33	36	40	43
Bicycling 6 mph (10 km/h) or 9-1/2 minute mile* 9 mph (15 km/h) or 6-1/2 minute mile*	23 36	26 41	29 46	33 50	36 55	39 60	42 65
Running 5 mph (8km/h) or 12 minute mile* 6 mph (10 km/h) or 9-1/2 minute mile*	60 73	66 79	72 85	78 92	84 100	90 107	95 113
Soccer	63	72	81	90	99	108	117
Swimming 33 yards/minute (30 m/m) or 54 minute mile* Breast Front crawl Back	 34 43 30	 38 49 34	 43 56 38	 48 62 42	 53 68 47	 58 74 51	 62 80 55
Tennis	39	44	50	55	61	66	72
Walking 2-1/2 mph (4 km/h) or 24 minute mile* 3-1/2 mph (6 km/h) or 16 minute mile*	23 30	26 32	28 34	30 37	32 40	34 43	36 48

* For ease of comparison, pounds, miles per hour (mph), kilometers per hour (km/h) and minutes per mile are rounded as they relate to calories burned.

Summary: Let's Go!

Knitting it together: stretching, cardio and resistance training ... oh, and eating right, too!

> **Develop your own fitness plan** and attach to it the same importance you give school, work and play. Your body deserves it!

It's important to distill all the information into a working plan for yourself. All training programs should include stretching, cardiovascular exercise and resistance training. Fuel yourself with good food and develop intelligent eating habits.

● Stretch those muscles to be exercised each day before and after each workout.

Goal: Serious flexibility training involves 30 minutes of stretching 3 times each week.

● Exercise within your target heart rate zone 3-4 times a week in 20-40 minute sessions.

Goal: We recommend you train at the high end of your target zone for at least 30 minutes 4 times each week.

● Exercise those muscles of the core or sport-specific programs 2-3 times a week making sure you rest 1 day before days you work the same muscles.

Goals: Advance 2 weight levels in each exercise of a

core muscle development program. Then ditto for a sport-specific program(s) if you are so inclined.

● Eat a variety of nourishing foods on a regular basis.

Goal: Make grains, vegetables and fruits the foundation of all your meals.

● Develop a plan and a weekly chart of exercises in order to track progress. It may behoove you to chart what you eat as well. Try keeping a journal of all your day's activities as well as your passing thoughts and feelings.

Goal: Chart the next 6 weeks of an exercise program, noting exercises performed and weight lifted.

And finally ...
Does making fitness goals and working to fulfill them still seem like a big load? Ask yourself how many hours a day you spend at school, doing homework, working and running errands? It's a lot, isn't it? These are activities you may not really have fun with, either. But you keep at them to keep yourself afloat.

Why not make room for something every bit as important as that and more — your healthy body!

Resources

BOOKS / READING
Journal writing
Wilber, Jessica. *Totally Private & Personal: Journaling Ideas for Girls and Young Women.* Minneapolis, Minnesota: Free Spirit Publishing.

Issues / fitness
Schwager, Tina. *The Right Moves: A Girl's Guide to Getting Fit and Feeling Good.* Minneapolis, Minnesota: Free Spirit Publishing, 1998.

Nutrition
Dietary Guidelines for Americans, 2000.
United States Department of Agriculture and the United States Department of Health and Human Services.

To download this guide (Item 147-G, $4.75 per copy) www.usda.gov/cnpp or call 888-878-3256 (Federal Consumer Information Center)

Puberty
Drill, Esther. *Deal WIth It! A Whole New Approach to Your Body, Brain, and Life as a Gurl.* Pocket Books, 1999.

Stretching
Anderson, Bob. *Stretching.* Bolinas, California: Shelter Publications, Inc., 2000.

Other titles for girls
Free Spirit Publishing Inc.
400 First Avenue North
Suite 616

Minneapolis, MN 55401-1724
800-735-7323
help4kids@freespirit.com
www.freespirit.com

EQUIPMENT
Most sporting goods stores have weight training equipment. Stores who specialize in fitness merchandise may have higher quality stuff.

Check out:
Fitness Resource
www.fitnessresource.com

Busy Bodies
www.busybodies.com

Heart rate monitors
Polar heart rate monitors
www.polarusa.com

MAGAZINES
General subscriptions
www.magazania.com

Fitness
PO Box 5309
Harlan, IA 51593-2809
1-800-888-1181
www.fitness.com

Jump
PO Box 55954
Boulder, CO 80323-5954
1-888-369-JUMP

Seventeen
711 Third Avenue
19th Floor
New York, NY 10017
www.seventeen.com

YM
375 Lexington Avenue
New York, NY 10017-5514
www.ym.com

WEB SITES
Puberty
www.beinggirl.com

Health and fitness
American Academy
of Pediatrics
www.app.org

American Heart Association
www.americanheart.org

American Council on Exercise
www.acefitness.org

Center for Disease Control
www.cdc.gov

Health Magazine
www.health.com

www.kidshealth.org

www.medem.com

www.my.webmd.com

Nutrition
American Dietetic Association
www.eatright.org

Food and Nutrition
Information Center
www.nal.usda.gov

U.S. Department of
Agriculture
www.usda.gov

General
!Girl Power!
Campaign Homepage
www.health.org/gpower/

The Just For Girls Web Site
www.girlscouts.org/girls/

Seventeen Magazine
www.seventeen.com

Bibliography

Anderson, Bob. *Stretching.* Bolinas, California: Shelter Publications, Inc., 2000.

Doren, Kim. *You Go Girl! Winning the Women's Way.* Kansas City, Missouri: Andrews McMeel Publishing, 2000.

Greenberg-Lake: The Analysis Group. *Shortchanging Girls, Shortchanging America, Executive Summary.* Washington, DC: AAUW Educational Foundation, 1994.

Haag, Pamela. *Voices of a Generation: Teenage Girls on Sex, School, and Self.* Washington, DC: AAUW Educational Foundation, 1999.

Litt, Ann Selkowitz. *The College Student's Guide to Eating Well on Campus.* Bethesda, Maryland: Tulip Hill Press, 2000.

Nutrition and Your Health: Dietary Guidelines for Americans, 5th Edition, 2000: United States Department of Agriculture and the United States Department of Health and Human Services, 2000.

Schwager, Tina. *The Right Moves: A Girl's Guide to Getting Fit and Feeling Good.* Minneapolis, Minnesota: Free Spirit Publishing, 1998.

Sullivan, Andy, M.D. *Care of the Young Athlete.* American Academy of Orthopedic Surgeons and American Academy of Pediatrics, 2000.

Wolf, Naomi. *The Beauty Myth: How Images of Beauty Are Used Against Women.* New York, New York: William Morrow and Company, Inc., 1991.

Youngs, Jennifer Leigh. *Feeling Great, Looking Hot & Loving Yourself!.* Dearfield Beach, Florida: Health Communications, Inc., 2000.

Index

Authors and Illustrator

Katrina Gaede is a 5-time California State Champion gymnast, a member of two national championship cheerleading squads and former California Head Instructor for the National Cheerleaders Association. Katrina holds a B.A. in Exercise Physiology, is a certified nutritional expert and currently works as a certified personal trainer in La Jolla, California.

Alan Lachica is a certified personal trainer and USA Amateur Boxing coach. His clients have included top professional athletes in Major League Baseball and the National Football League. His boxing exhibitions have been featured on local and national television, including Eye on America (CBS News). He is a graduate of Cal State Long Beach and currently lives in La Jolla, California, with wife Lynn and daughter Camryn.

Doug Werner is the author of the internationally acclaimed Start-Up Sports series. In previous lifetimes he graduated with a fine arts degree from Cal State Long Beach, built an ad agency and founded a graphics firm. In 1994 he established Tracks Publishing. Doug lives with his wife Kathleen and daughter Joy in San Diego, California — one of the major sport funzones on the planet.

Cristina Martinez is a national award-winning illustrator for The San Diego Union-Tribune. She is a graduate of Ringling School of Art and Design and worked as a news artist for the St. Petersburg Times before settling in San Diego. Cristina has won several awards from both Society of Newspaper Design and Society of Professional Journalists including Best of the West.